Traditional
BRITISH
~ Cooking ~

Traditional
BRITISH
~ Cooking ~

The best of British cooking:
a definitive collection.

Consultant Editor: Hilaire Walden

SELECT
EDITIONS

Select Editions imprint specially produced for Selectabook Ltd

Produced by Anness Publishing Ltd
Hermes House, 88–89 Blackfriars Road, London SE1 8HA
tel. 020 7401 2077; fax 020 7633 9499

www.annesspublishing.com

If you like the images in this book and would like to investigate using them for publishing,
promotions or advertising, please visit our website www.practicalpictures.com for more
information.

A CIP catalogue record for this book is available from the British Library.

Publisher: Joanna Lorenz
Senior Cookery Editor: Linda Fraser
Editor: Margaret Malone
Designer: Ian Sandom and Tony Paine
Photographers: Karl Adamson, David Armstrong, Steve Baxter,
James Duncan and Amanda Heywood
Additional Recipes: Alex Barker, Carla Capalbo, Sarah Gates,
Shirley Gill, Peter Jordan, Sue Maggs, Janice Murfitt, Louise Pickford, Laura Washburn and
Steven Wheeler

ETHICAL TRADING POLICY
Because of our ongoing ecological investment programme, you, as our customer, can have the
pleasure and reassurance of knowing that a tree is being cultivated on your behalf to naturally
replace the materials used to make the book you are holding. For further information about this
scheme, go to www.annesspublishing.com/trees

For all recipes, quantities are given in both metric and imperial measures and,
where appropriate, measures are also given in standard cups and spoons. Follow
one set, but not a mixture, because they are not interchangeable.
Standard spoon and cup measures are level:
1 tsp = 5ml, 1 tbsp = 15ml, 1 cup = 250ml/8fl oz
Size 3 (medium) eggs should be used unless otherwise stated.

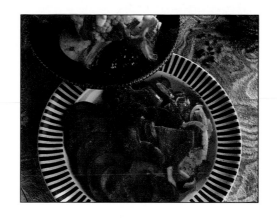

CONTENTS

INTRODUCTION

In recent years there has been a huge upsurge of interest in traditional British cooking. When nouvelle cuisine died – of starvation no doubt – it was replaced by a yearning for the simple yet supremely satisfying dishes for which these islands are deservedly famous: robust roasts, mouthwatering meat pies, perfect pastries and indulgent puddings.

Nostalgia for nursery food sent hundreds scurrying to restaurants renowned for mulligatawny soup, country meat loaf, baked rice pudding, or apple brown Betty, and when younger food-lovers raved about baked brioche with vine fruits, they little knew that what they claimed as a daring discovery was in fact an upmarket version of good old-fashioned bread and butter pudding.

A NATION OF MEAT EATERS

The British have always been great meat eaters, and it was in these islands that the technique of roasting on the spit was perfected. Roast beef remains a symbol of Britishness, and many households still celebrate Sunday lunch with the traditional roast joint. The combination of tender roast pork with crisp crackling and tangy apple sauce is one of life's pleasures, and roast lamb with mint sauce is another.

BEEF

British beef is on sale throughout the year, but it is more plentiful in the autumn. It is important to choose the right cut when cooking: ask your butcher or consult the list below:

BRISKET: Suitable for braising or boiling, brisket is sold on the bone or

Above: Beef Olives – beef slices with a bacon and mushroom filling.

boned and rolled. It is often salted.

CHUCK, THICK FLANK AND BLADE: Fairly lean, boneless cuts suitable for braising and stewing.

FILLET: The whole fillet is a luxury cut, traditionally used for Beef Wellington. Fillet steaks are extremely tender.

RIB ROAST: This large joint on the bone is a prime cut for roasting. It has plenty of marbling, making it moist and succulent.

RUMP STEAK: Not as tender as fillet, but full of flavour, this is excellent for grilling, frying or barbecuing.

SHIN AND LEG: Lean meat with plenty of connective tissue, these cuts are ideal for stocks, soups and casseroles.

SILVERSIDE: Originally, silverside was always salted, and formed the basis for the famous boiled beef and carrots. When sold fresh, it can be roasted, but it needs constant basting because it is so lean. It makes a good pot-roast.

SIRLOIN: Ideal for roasting, this juicy joint is sold on or off the bone. Also excellent as steaks.

TOPSIDE: Very lean and boneless, this is popular for roasting, although it is not as tender as sirloin. Topside steaks form the basis of beef olives.

Left: Beef Wellington and Squab Pie.

LAMB

Plentiful in the autumn, but most sought after in spring, when the new season's lamb comes on to the market.
BREAST: A fairly fatty cut, this is usually sold boned and rolled. Short ribs cut from the breast (riblets) are good for marinating and barbecuing.
CHUMP CHOPS: Flavoursome and tender, boneless ones are sold as steaks.
LEG: Whole or half leg joints are delicious for roasting; in Britain, rosemary is traditionally tucked under the skin. Leg steaks can be grilled, fried or barbecued but are very lean; baste them frequently.
LOIN CHOPS: Single or double (Barnsley chops), these are delicious grilled.
NECK: Cuts include best end – a roasting joint with six or seven rib bones (also sold as chops); middle neck, a bony cut for casseroling, and the neck fillet, a lean, tender muscle, which is good for kebabs.
SHOULDER: Whole shoulders have fine flavour and are good for roasting. Often sold boned and rolled.

PORK

Salted, pickled or fresh, pork has an ancient history in the British Isles. Available all year, it is now bred to be

Below: Hearty Lamb and Spring Vegetable Stew.

Above: Farmhouse Venison Pie – simple and satisfying.

leaner than in the past.
BACON: It is believed that the Romans brought the art of curing bacon with them when they invaded Britain in 55 BC. The preserved meat was a godsend during the long, harsh winters, when other meat was not available, and it has been beloved of Britons ever since. Green bacon is the unsmoked product. Sweet cured bacon has had a sweetener such as treacle or brown sugar added to the brine during curing. Bacon, gammon and ham are all terms for cured pork; gammon usually refers to the uncooked cured meat and ham to the cooked, but the definition is by no means clearcut.
BELLY: Slices are fairly fatty, but taste good when grilled until crisp and served with red cabbage.
CHUMP CHOPS: Sold with the bone or as steaks, these are good for grilling, frying or barbecuing. The meat is lean, so it may need basting.
FILLET: Boneless and very tender, this is good for stir-frying or rapid roasting. Low in fat, so needs to be kept moist.
HAND: From the lower part of the shoulder, this boned and rolled joint is good value for roasting. It is also cubed for casseroling. Shoulder spare rib chops are good for braising.
LEG: Sold as two joints – fillet or shank end. The British have always loved crackling, made by rubbing the rind with oil and salt before starting off the cooking at a high heat.
LOIN: The joint is good for roasting, but needs added moisture in the form of a marinade or fruit stuffing. Loin chops are very popular.
SPARE RIBS: Cut from the belly, these are single rib bones with a little meat left on. Ideal for marinating and baking or grilling, they can be parboiled first for extra tenderness.

GAME

Game – not always legally acquired – has long been an accepted part of the British diet. While the wealthy dined on venison and pheasant, the peasants plumped for rabbit or pigeon pie. In Britain, wild game may only be shot at certain times of the year, outside the nesting and mating seasons for each species. Game birds include grouse (August 12 to December 10); pheasant (October 1 to February 1); wild duck (September 1 to January 31) and pigeon (available all year). Quail may not be shot in the wild but is farmed. The season for venison varies according to the species and the area. Hare is in season from August 1 to March 31. Rabbit is available all year.

FISH FROM RIVER AND SEA

Rivers and the encircling sea have always provided these islands with plenty of fish and shellfish, and, although factory ships and fast-freezing techniques have changed the picture considerably, it is still possible to buy fresh cod or mackerel from a fisherman who has just landed his catch.

SEA FISH

These are classified in three groups: white fish, oily fish and shellfish. The former includes coley and cod; large round fish usually sold as steaks, cutlets or fillets. Smaller round fish include whiting and haddock. Halibut and turbot are large flat fish, generally sold as steaks or fillets, while smaller flat fish like plaice, lemon sole or Dover sole are served whole or as fillets. Oily fish are so called because their oil is dispersed throughout the flesh, rather than being confined to the liver. Herring and mackerel are prime examples.

Britain boasts some of the world's finest shellfish, including crab, lobsters, crawfish, Dublin Bay prawns and mussels. Shrimps are widely available – the brown ones are a particular delicacy – and prawns are caught in the northern waters. Traditionally, Britain's most famous shellfish are probably cockles, winkles and whelks, once widely sold on stalls and fishmonger's slabs, but today usually sold bottled in vinegar.

FRESHWATER FISH

Britain's most famous freshwater fish, salmon, is now widely farmed, but connoisseurs prefer wild Scottish salmon, which is at its best from May to July. Other popular freshwater fish include carp, perch, pike and trout.

SMOKED FISH

Britain has a long tradition of smoking both freshwater fish (salmon and trout) and sea fish. The latter category includes smoked haddock; the most well known variety being the straw-coloured finnan haddock from the village of Findon. Glasgow Pales are small haddock with a faint smoky flavour, while Arbroath Smokies are hot smoked haddock or whiting.

Above: Leeks with Mustard Dressing.

A FEAST OF FRUIT AND VEGETABLES

Visitors to Britain often remark on the quality and variety of vegetables and fruit available from country markets and pick-your-own farms. The range wasn't always as vast as it is today: in medieval times cabbages, onions, leeks and garlic (a gift from the Romans) were just about the only vegetables grown, and their use was largely restricted to flavouring soups and meat dishes. At that time, apples, cherries and plums were the most common fruit. As the centuries passed and Britain became a great trading nation (and a nation of gardeners), fruit and vegetables were grown in greater numbers and new varieties arrived from overseas. Potatoes were greeted with particular enthusiasm and soon supplanted parsnips in popularity. They continue to be a very important part of the British diet, in such dishes as shepherd's pie, Lancashire hotpot and Irish stew.

Today, British cooks have access to fruit and vegetables from all over the world, but still set store by seasonal specialities, like home-grown asparagus, which reaches the farm stalls just as the first new potatoes arrive in late spring. Summer is celebrated with

Left: Herrings in Oatmeal with Mustard and Fish and Chips.

strawberries, the traditional treat of tennis spectators at Wimbledon, and autumn sees scores of walkers searching for the finest blackberries.

We continue to cling to our roots – onions, leeks, carrots, beetroot, potatoes, celeriac, parsnips, swedes and turnips – while enjoying an ever-widening range of salad leaves. Eating greens is a British institution, and spinach, Brussels sprouts, broccoli, cabbage and curly kale remain as popular as ever. Podding peas is one of the delights of childhood, and, although the frozen pea is a huge asset, there's nothing like the experience of easing a pod apart and savouring the sweet green peas inside.

Tomatoes are relative newcomers to Britain, having been introduced towards the end of the eighteenth century. Today they are among our most popular ingredients, especially when picked straight from the plant. The British fruit bowl is filled all year round, with apples, apricots, cherries, pears, peaches, plums and all the glorious soft fruits, including strawberries, raspberries, currants and gooseberries. Rhubarb and quinces are old favourites that feature in some of the earliest recipe books.

Below: Basic household dry goods.

Above: The quintessential savoury snack – Macaroni and Blue Cheese.

DELIGHTS FROM THE DAIRY

Milk, butter and cheese have been a central part of the British diet for the past 2000 years. Until the nineteenth century, cheese was made on the farm, usually by the farmer's wife and daughters, with very simple equipment.

Traditional British cheeses take their names from their places of origin. The main varieties of traditional hard cheese still marketed today are Caerphilly, Cheddar, Cheshire, Derby, Double Gloucester, Lancashire, Red Leicester, Stilton and Wensleydale.

THE WELL-STOCKED PANTRY

The pantry was once an essential adjunct to every well-equipped kitchen. With the arrival of fitted units and larder cupboards, pantries all but disappeared, but many cooks mourn their passing and are clamouring for their return. A well-stocked British pantry would include:
• flour (plain, self-raising and wholemeal); also cornflour
• raising agents like baking powder, bicarbonate of soda and easy-blend dried yeast
• sugar (granulated, caster, brown and icing); also golden syrup, honey and treacle
• dried fruit (currants, raisins, sultanas, dates); also ready-to-eat dried apricots and prunes
• nuts, particularly almonds and walnuts, bought in small quantities and regularly replenished
• a small stock of dried herbs (British cooks traditionally use fresh) and spices, especially nutmeg, cinnamon, cloves, ground ginger and mixed spice
• sauces, especially Worcestershire sauce and mushroom ketchup
• oils and vinegars, including raspberry vinegar
• rice, particularly pudding rice (short-grain) and pasta, especially macaroni

With such a wealth of wonderful ingredients, it is no wonder that traditional British cooking tends to be simple. Sauces are seldom used to mask foods, but rather to provide a sharp contrast or subtle emphasis.
At its best, traditional British food is unbeatable. The recipes in this book are proof of that, and will delight both those who remember many of these dishes, and those for whom traditional British cooking is a recent discovery.

SOUPS

Britain's rich tradition of soup-making encompasses a wide range of different recipes, from light Country Vegetable Soup to warming Split Pea and Bacon Soup, from fragrant puréed Green Pea and Mint Soup to savoury Smoked Haddock and Potato Soup and spicy Mulligatawny. There are also hearty meat-and-vegetable dishes that are akin to stews, such as Cock-a-leekie and Scotch Broth. Many of the soups evolved in the past as staple foods of the poor, often eaten with bread as the main part of a meal. Today, too, a soup can form the core of a light, convenient lunch or supper. Alternatively, serve soups as the first course of a meal, following the practice established in Victorian times.

GREEN PEA AND MINT SOUP

This soup is equally delicious cold. Instead of reheating it after puréeing, leave it to cool and then chill lightly in the fridge. Stir in the swirl of cream just before serving.

INGREDIENTS

Serves 4
50g/2oz/4 tbsp butter
4 spring onions (scallions), chopped
450g/1 lb fresh or frozen peas
600ml/1 pint/2½ cups chicken or
  vegetable stock
2 large mint sprigs
600 ml/1 pint/2½ cups milk
pinch of sugar (optional)
salt and pepper
single cream, to serve
small mint sprigs, to garnish

1 Heat the butter in a large saucepan, add the spring onions (scallions), and cook gently until softened but not coloured.

2 Stir the peas into the pan, add the stock and mint and bring to the boil. Cover and simmer very gently for about 30 minutes for fresh peas or 15 minutes if you are using frozen peas, until the peas are very tender. Remove about 45ml/3 tbsp of the peas using a slotted spoon, and reserve for the garnish.

FREEZER NOTE
The soup can be frozen for up to two months after step 2. Allow it to thaw in the fridge before puréeing and reheating.

3 Pour the soup into a food processor or blender, add the milk and purée until smooth. Then return the soup to the pan and reheat gently. Season to taste, adding a pinch of sugar, if liked.

4 Pour the soup into bowls. Swirl a little cream into each, then garnish with mint and the reserved peas.

LEEK AND POTATO SOUP

The chopped vegetables in this recipe produce a chunky soup. If you prefer a smooth texture, press the mixture through a sieve (strainer) or purée it in a food mill.

INGREDIENTS

Serves 4
50g/2oz/4 tbsp butter
2 leeks, chopped
1 small onion, finely chopped
350g/12oz potatoes, chopped
900ml/1½ pints/3¾ cups chicken or
  vegetable stock
salt and pepper

1 Heat 25g/1oz/2 tbsp of the butter in a large saucepan, add the leeks and onions and cook gently, stirring occasionally, for about 7 minutes, until softened but not browned.

COOK'S TIP
Don't use a food processor to purée this soup as it can give the potatoes a gluey consistency.

2 Add the potatoes to the pan and cook, stirring occasionally, for 2–3 minutes, then add the stock and bring to the boil. Cover the pan and simmer gently for 30–35 minutes, until the vegetables are very tender.

3 Adjust the seasoning, remove the pan from the heat and stir in the remaining butter in small pieces. Serve hot with crusty bread.

COCK-A-LEEKIE

This ancient soup recipe – it is known from as long ago as 1598 – originally included beef as well as chicken. In the past it would have been made from an old cock bird, hence the name.

INGREDIENTS

Serves 4–6
2 chicken portions, about 275g/10oz
*   each*
1.2 litres/2 pints/5 cups chicken stock
bouquet garni
4 leeks
8–12 prunes, soaked
salt and pepper
soft buttered rolls, to serve

1 Gently cook the chicken, stock and bouquet garni for 40 minutes.

2 Cut the white part of the leeks into 2.5cm/1in slices and thinly slice a little of the green part.

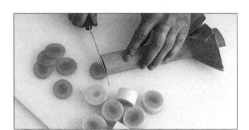

3 Add the white part of the leeks and the prunes to the saucepan and cook gently for 20 minutes, then add the green part of the leeks and cook for a further 10–15 minutes.

4 Discard the bouquet garni. Remove the chicken from the pan, discard the skin and bones and chop the flesh. Return the chicken to the pan and season the soup. Heat the soup through, then serve hot with soft buttered rolls.

SCOTCH BROTH

Sustaining and warming, Scotch Broth is custom-made for chilly Scottish weather, and makes a delicious winter soup anywhere.

INGREDIENTS

Serves 6–8
1kg/2 lb lean neck of lamb, cut into
*   large, even-sized chunks*
1.75 litres/3 pints/7½ cups water
1 large onion, chopped
50g/2oz/¼ cup pearl barley
bouquet garni
1 large carrot, chopped
1 turnip, chopped
3 leeks, chopped
½ small white cabbage, shredded
salt and pepper

1 Put the lamb and water into a large saucepan and bring to the boil. Skim off the scum, then stir in the onion, barley and bouquet garni.

2 Bring the soup back to the boil, then partly cover the saucepan and simmer gently for 1 hour. Add the remaining vegetables and the seasoning to the pan. Bring to the boil, partly cover again and simmer for about 35 minutes until the vegetables are tender.

3 Remove surplus fat from the top of the soup, then serve hot, sprinkled with chopped parsley.

TOMATO AND BLUE CHEESE SOUP

INGREDIENTS

Serves 4

1.5kg/3lb ripe tomatoes, peeled, quartered, and seeded
2 garlic cloves, finely chopped
30ml/2 tbsp vegetable oil
1 leek, chopped
1 carrot, chopped
1 litre/1¾ pints/4 cups unsalted chicken stock
115g/4oz blue cheese, cut into smallish pieces
45ml/3 tbsp single cream
a few fresh basil leaves, plus extra for garnishing
175g/6oz bacon, cooked and crumbled
salt and black pepper

1 Preheat the oven to 200°C/400°F/ Gas 6. Spread the tomatoes in a shallow baking dish with the garlic.

2 Add seasoning to taste and bake for about 35 minutes.

3 Heat the oil in a large saucepan. Add the leek and carrot and season lightly with salt and pepper. Cook over a low heat for 10 minutes, stirring occasionally, until softened.

4 Stir in the stock and tomatoes. Bring to the boil, then lower the heat, cover and simmer for 20 minutes.

5 Add the blue cheese, cream and basil. Transfer to a food processor or blender and process until smooth, working in batches if necessary. Taste and adjust the seasoning.

6 Reheat the soup, but do not boil. Ladle into bowls and garnish with the crumbled bacon and basil.

MUSHROOM AND HERB POTTAGE

Although you can make mushroom soup with a nice smooth texture, it is more time consuming and you waste a lot of mushrooms – so enjoy the slightly nutty consistency instead!

───── INGREDIENTS ─────

Serves 4
50g/2oz smoked streaky bacon
1 white onion, chopped
15ml/1 tbsp sunflower oil
350g/12oz flat cap field mushrooms or
  a mixture of wild and brown
  mushrooms
600ml/1 pint/2½ cups good meat stock
30ml/2 tbsp sweet sherry
30ml/2 tbsp chopped, mixed fresh
  herbs, such as sage, rosemary, thyme
  or marjoram, or 10ml/2 tsp dried
salt and black pepper
60ml/4 tbsp thick Greek-style yogurt or
  crème fraîche and a few sprigs of
  marjoram or sage, to garnish

1 Roughly chop the bacon and place in a large saucepan. Cook gently until all the fat comes out of the bacon.

2 Add the onion and soften, adding oil if necessary. Wipe the mushrooms clean, roughly chop and add to the pan. Cover and sweat until they have completely softened and their liquid has run out.

3 Add the stock, sherry, herbs and seasoning, cover and simmer for 10-12 minutes. Blend or liquidise the soup until smooth, but don't worry if you still have a slightly textured result.

4 Check the seasoning and heat through. Serve with a dollop of yogurt or crème fraîche and a herb sprig in each bowl.

COUNTRY VEGETABLE SOUP

To ring the changes, vary the vegetables according to what is in season.

INGREDIENTS

Serves 4

50g/2oz/4 tbsp butter
1 onion, chopped
2 leeks, sliced
2 celery sticks, sliced
2 carrots, sliced
2 small turnips, chopped
4 ripe tomatoes, skinned and chopped
1 litre/1¾ pints/4 cups chicken, veal or
   vegetable stock
bouquet garni
115g/4oz green beans, chopped
salt and pepper
chopped herbs such as tarragon,
   thyme, chives and parsley, to garnish

1 Heat the butter in a large saucepan, add the onion and leeks and cook gently until soft but not coloured.

2 Add the celery, carrots and turnips and cook for 3–4 minutes, stirring occasionally. Stir in the tomatoes and stock, add the bouquet garni and simmer for about 20 minutes.

3 Add the beans to the soup and cook until all the vegetables are tender. Season to taste and serve garnished with chopped herbs.

SPLIT PEA AND BACON SOUP

Another name for this soup is 'London Particular', from the dense fogs for which the city used to be notorious. The fogs in turn were named 'pea-soupers'.

INGREDIENTS

Serves 4

15g/½oz/1 tbsp butter
115g/4oz smoked back bacon,
   chopped
1 large onion, chopped
1 carrot, chopped
1 celery stick, chopped
75g/3oz/scant ½ cup split peas
1.2 litres/2 pints/5 cups chicken stock
salt and pepper
2 thick slices firm bread, buttered and
   without crusts
2 slices streaky bacon

1 Heat the butter in a saucepan, add the back bacon and cook until the fat runs. Stir in the onion, carrot and celery and cook for 2–3 minutes.

2 Add the split peas followed by the stock. Bring to the boil, stirring occasionally, then cover and simmer for 45–60 minutes.

3 Meanwhile, preheat the oven to 180°C/350°F/Gas 4 and bake the bread for about 20 minutes, until crisp and brown, then cut into cubes.

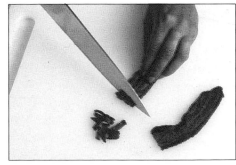

4 Grill the streaky bacon until very crisp, then chop finely.

5 When the soup is ready, season to taste and serve hot with chopped bacon and croutons scattered on each portion.

SMOKED HADDOCK AND POTATO SOUP

The traditional name for this
soup is 'cullen skink'. A cullen is
the 'seatown' or port district of
a town, while 'skink' means
stock or broth.

INGREDIENTS

Serves 6
1 Finnan haddock, about 350g/12oz
1 onion, chopped
bouquet garni
900ml/1½ pints/3¾ cups water
500g/1¼ lb potatoes, quartered
600ml/1 pint/2½ cups milk
40g/1½oz/3 tbsp butter
salt and pepper
snipped chives, to garnish

1 Put the haddock, onion, bouquet
garni and water into a large
saucepan and bring to the boil. Skim
the scum from the surface, then cover
the pan. Reduce the heat and poach for
10–15 minutes, until the haddock
flakes easily.

2 Lift the haddock from the pan,
using a fish slice, and remove the
skin and bones. Flake the flesh and
reserve. Return the skin and bones to
the pan and simmer, uncovered, for
30 minutes.

3 Strain the fish stock and return to
the pan, then add the potatoes and
simmer for about 25 minutes, or until
tender. Remove the potatoes from the
pan using a slotted spoon. Add the
milk to the pan and bring to the boil.

4 Meanwhile, mash the potatoes with
the butter, then whisk into the milk
in the pan until thick and creamy. Add
the flaked fish to the pan and adjust
the seasoning. Sprinkle with chives and
serve at once with crusty bread.

MULLIGATAWNY SOUP

Mulligatawny (which means 'pepper water') was introduced into England in the late eighteenth century by members of the army and colonial service returning home from India.

---INGREDIENTS---

Serves 4

50g/2oz/4 tbsp butter or 60ml/4 tbsp
  oil
2 large chicken joints, about 350g/
  12oz each
1 onion, chopped
1 carrot, chopped
1 small turnip, chopped
about 15ml/1 tbsp curry powder,
  to taste
4 cloves
6 black peppercorns, lightly crushed
50g/2oz/¼ cup lentils
900ml/1½ pints/3¾ cups chicken stock
40g/1½oz/¼ cup sultanas (golden
  raisins)
salt and pepper

1 Melt the butter or heat the oil in a large saucepan, then brown the chicken over a brisk heat. Transfer the chicken to a plate.

COOK'S TIP
Choose red split lentils for the best colour, although either green or brown lentils could also be used.

2 Add the onion, carrot and turnip to the pan and cook, stirring occasionally, until lightly coloured. Stir in the curry powder, cloves and peppercorns and cook for 1–2 minutes, then add the lentils.

3 Pour the stock into the pan, bring to the boil, then add the sultanas (golden raisins) and chicken and any juices from the plate. Cover and simmer gently for about 1¼ hours.

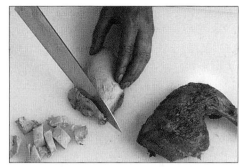

4 Remove the chicken from the pan and discard the skin and bones. Chop the flesh, return to the soup and reheat. Check the seasoning before serving the soup piping hot.

CHICKEN BROTH WITH CHEESE TOASTS

INGREDIENTS

Serves 4

1 roasted chicken carcase
1 onion, quartered
2 celery sticks, finely chopped
1 garlic clove, crushed
few sprigs parsley
2 bay leaves
225g/8oz can chopped tomatoes
½ x 400g/14oz can chick-peas
30–45ml/2–3 tbsp leftover vegetables,
  chopped, or 1 large carrot, finely
  chopped
15ml/1 tbsp chopped fresh parsley
2 slices toast
25g/1oz/¼ cup grated cheese
salt and black pepper

1 Pick off any little bits of flesh from the carcase, especially from the underside where there is often some very tasty dark meat. Put aside.

2 Place the carcase, broken in half, in a large pan with the onion, half the celery, the garlic, herbs and sufficient water to cover. Cover the pan, bring to the boil and simmer for about 30 minutes, or until you are left with about 300ml/½ pint/1¼ cups of liquid.

3 Strain the stock and return to the pan. Add the chicken flesh, the remaining celery, the tomatoes, chick-peas (and their liquid), vegetables and parsley. Season to taste and simmer for another 7–10 minutes.

4 Meanwhile, sprinkle the toast with the cheese and grill until bubbling. Cut the toast into fingers or quarters and serve with, or floating on top of, the finished soup.

BREAD AND CHEESE SOUP

INGREDIENTS

Serves 4

115g/4oz strong-flavoured or blue
  cheese, or 175g/6oz mild cheese
600ml/1 pint/2½ cups semi-skimmed
  milk
few pinches ground mace
4–6 slices stale bread
30ml/2 tbsp olive oil
1 large garlic clove, crushed
salt and black pepper
15ml/1 tbsp snipped chives, to garnish

1 Remove any rinds from the cheese and grate into a heavy-based, preferably non-stick pan. Add the milk and heat through very slowly, stirring frequently to make sure it does not stick and burn.

2 When all the cheese has melted, add the mace, seasoning, and one piece of crustless bread. Cook over a very gentle heat until the bread has softened and slightly thickened the soup.

3 Mix the oil with the garlic and brush over the remaining bread. Toast until crisp, then cut into triangles or fingers. Sprinkle the soup with chives and serve with the toast.

COOK'S TIP
Don't mix blue cheeses with other kinds of cheese in this soup.

STARTERS AND SNACKS

Recipes suitable for present-day first courses and snacks are culled from a variety of traditional sources. Potting and smoking fish were methods of preserving developed in the days before refrigeration, providing us with Potted Shrimps and several delicious smoked fish recipes. There are regional specialities such as Welsh Rabbit, and dishes like Stuffed Mushrooms that make use of seasonal foods. A number of the dishes used to be breakfast fare – among them Devilled Kidneys – while others, such as Savoury Scrambled Eggs and Mussels In Bacon, used to be served as 'savouries' to round off a formal dinner.

ENGLISH PLOUGHMAN'S PÂTÉ

INGREDIENTS

Serves 4

50g/2oz/3 tbsp full fat soft cheese
50g/2oz/¾ cup grated Caerphilly cheese
50g/2oz/¾ cup grated Double
  Gloucester cheese
4 silverskin pickled onions, drained and
  finely chopped
15ml/1 tbsp apricot chutney
25g/1oz/2 tbsp butter, melted
30ml/2 tbsp snipped fresh chives
salt and black pepper
4 slices soft grain bread
watercress and cherry tomatoes,
  to serve

1 Mix together the soft cheese, grated cheeses, onions, chutney and butter in a bowl and season lightly.

2 Spoon the mixture on to a sheet of greaseproof paper and roll up into a cylinder, smoothing the mixture into a roll with your hands. Scrunch the ends of the paper together and twist to seal. Pop in the freezer for about 30 minutes, until just firm.

3 Spread the chives on a plate, then unwrap the chilled cheese pâté. Roll in the chives until evenly coated. Wrap in clear film and chill for 10 minutes.

4 Preheat the grill. Toast the bread lightly on both sides. Cut off the crusts and slice each piece in half horizontally. Cut each half into two triangles. Grill, untoasted side up, until golden and curled at the edges.

5 Slice the pâté into rounds and serve three or four rounds per person with the Melba toast, watercress and cherry tomatoes.

SMOKED MACKEREL AND APPLE DIP

Serve this quick, fishy dip with tasty, curried dippers.

INGREDIENTS

Serves 6–8
350g/12oz smoked mackerel, skinned
    and boned
1 soft eating apple, peeled, cored and
    cut into chunks
150ml/¼ pint/⅔ cup fromage frais
pinch paprika or curry powder
salt and black pepper
apple slices, to garnish

For the curried dippers
4 slices white bread, crusts removed
25g/1oz/2 tbsp butter, softened
5ml/1 tsp curry paste

1 Place the smoked mackerel in a food processor with the apple, fromage frais and seasonings.

2 Blend for about 2 minutes or until the mixture is really smooth. Check the seasoning, transfer to a small serving dish and chill.

3 Preheat the oven to 200°C /400°F/ Gas 6. To make the curried dippers, place the bread on a baking sheet. Blend the butter and curry paste thoroughly, then spread over the bread.

4 Cook the bread in the oven for about 10 minutes, or until crisp and golden. Cut into fingers and serve, while still warm, with the dip, garnished with the apple slices.

COOK'S TIP
Instead of using plain sliced bread, try other breads for the dippers – Italian ciabatta, rye, or pitta breads would be excellent.

SMOKED TROUT SALAD

Horseradish is as good a partner to smoked trout as it is to roast beef. In this recipe it combines with yogurt to make a delicious light salad dressing.

INGREDIENTS

Serves 4

1 oakleaf or other red lettuce
225g/8oz small tomatoes, cut into thin wedges
½ cucumber, peeled and thinly sliced
4 smoked trout fillets, about 200g/7oz each, skinned and flaked

For The Dressing
pinch of English mustard powder
15–20ml/3–4 tsp white wine vinegar
30ml/2 tbsp light olive oil
100ml/3½ fl oz/scant ½ cup plain (natural) yogurt
about 30ml/2 tbsp grated fresh or bottled horseradish
pinch of caster (superfine) sugar

1 First, make the dressing. Mix together the mustard powder and vinegar, then gradually whisk in the oil, yogurt, horseradish and sugar. Set aside for 30 minutes.

COOK'S TIP
Salt should not be necessary in this recipe because of the saltiness of the smoked trout.

2 Place the lettuce leaves in a large bowl. Stir the dressing again, then pour half of it over the leaves and toss lightly using two spoons.

3 Arrange the lettuce on four individual plates with the tomatoes, cucumber and trout. Spoon over the remaining dressing and serve at once.

SMOKED HADDOCK PÂTÉ

Arbroath smokies are small haddock that are beheaded and gutted but not split before being salted and hot-smoked.

INGREDIENTS

Serves 6
*3 large Arbroath smokies, about 225g/
   8oz each*
*275g/10oz/1¼ cups medium fat soft
   cheese*
3 eggs, beaten
30–45ml/2–3 tbsp lemon juice
pepper
sprigs of chervil, to garnish
*lemon wedges and lettuce leaves,
   to serve*

1 Preheat the oven to 160°C/325°F/ Gas 3. Butter six ramekin dishes.

2 Lay the smokies in a baking dish and heat through in the oven for 10 minutes. Carefully remove the skin and bones from the smokies, then flake the flesh into a bowl.

COOK'S TIP
There should be no need to add salt to this recipe, as smoked haddock is naturally salty – taste the mixture to check.

3 Mash the fish with a fork and work in the cheese, then the eggs. Add lemon juice and pepper to taste.

4 Divide the fish mixture among the ramekins and place in a roasting tin. Pour hot water into the roasting tin to come halfway up the dishes. Bake for 30 minutes, until just set.

5 Allow to cool for 2–3 minutes, then run a knife point around the edge of each dish and invert on to a warmed plate. Garnish with chervil sprigs and serve with the lemon and lettuce.

PEARS AND STILTON

Stilton is the classic British blue cheese, but you could use blue Cheshire instead, or even a non-British cheese such as Gorgonzola.

INGREDIENTS

Serves 4
4 ripe pears, lightly chilled
75g/3oz blue Stilton cheese
50g/2oz curd (medium fat soft cheese)
pepper
watercress sprigs, to garnish

For The Dressing
45ml/3 tbsp light olive oil
15ml/1 tbsp lemon juice
10ml/½ tbsp toasted poppy seeds
salt and pepper

1 First make the dressing, place the olive oil, lemon juice, poppy seeds and seasoning in a screw-topped jar and shake together until emulsified.

2 Cut the pears in half lengthways, then scoop out the cores and cut away the calyx from the rounded end.

3 Beat together the Stilton, soft cheese and a little pepper. Divide this mixture among the cavities in the pears.

4 Shake the dressing to mix it again, then spoon it over the pears. Serve garnished with watercress.

POTTED SHRIMPS

The tiny brown shrimps traditionally used for potting are very fiddley to peel. Since they are rare nowadays, it is easier to use peeled cooked prawns (shrimps) instead.

INGREDIENTS

Serves 4
225g/8oz shelled shrimps
225g/8oz/1 cup butter
pinch of ground mace
salt
cayenne pepper
dill (dillweed) sprigs, to garnish
lemon wedges and thin slices of brown bread and butter, to serve

1 Chop a quarter of the shrimps. Melt 115g/4oz/½ cup of the butter slowly, carefully skimming off any foam that rises to the surface.

2 Stir all the shrimps, the mace, salt and cayenne into the pan and heat gently without boiling. Pour the shrimps and butter mixture into four individual pots and leave to cool.

3 Heat the remaining butter in a clean small saucepan, then carefully spoon the clear butter over the shrimps, leaving behind the sediment.

4 Leave until the butter is almost set, then place a dill (dillweed) sprig in the centre of each pot. Leave to set completely, then cover and chill.

5 Transfer the shrimps to room temperature 30 minutes before serving with lemon wedges and thin slices of brown bread and butter.

LEEK AND BROCCOLI TARTLETS

Serves 4

175g/6oz/1½ cups plain flour, sifted
115g/4oz/½ cup butter
25g/1oz finely grated pecorino cheese
  or young, mild Parmesan
2 small leeks, sliced
75g/3oz tiny broccoli florets
150ml/¼ pint/⅔ cup milk
2 eggs
30ml/2 tbsp double cream
few pinches ground mace
salt and black pepper
15g/½oz flaked almonds, toasted, to
  garnish

1 Blend the flour, butter and cheese together in a food processor to give a fine crumb consistency. Add salt to taste. Stir in 60–90ml/4–6 tbsp cold water and bring the pastry together in a ball. Chill for 15 minutes.

2 Preheat the oven to 190°C/375°F/ Gas 5. Roll out the pastry on a floured surface and use to line four 10cm/4in tartlet tins. Line the pastry cases with greaseproof paper and fill with baking beans. Bake the pastry cases blind for 15 minutes, then remove the paper and cook for a further 5 minutes to dry out the bases.

3 To make the filling, place the vegetables in a pan and cook them in the milk for 2–3 minutes. Strain the milk into a small bowl and whisk in the eggs, mace, seasoning and cream.

4 Arrange the vegetables in the pastry cases and pour over the egg mixture. Bake for 20 minutes, or until the filling is just firm. Sprinkle with almonds before serving.

> **COOK'S TIP**
> Cook and freeze the tartlet cases, ready for easy weekend meals. They only need 15 minutes defrosting. Use other colourful, crunchy vegetables in season.

MUSHROOM POPOVERS

Children usually love traditional Yorkshire puddings, so don't just serve them with roasts. Here is a quick mushroom filling, though leftover roast meat, chopped up with gravy, is also good.

──────── INGREDIENTS ────────

Serves 4
1 egg
115g/4oz/1 cup plain flour
300ml/½ pint/1¼ cups milk
pinch salt

For the filling
15ml/1 tbsp sunflower oil
115g/4oz mushrooms, sliced
few drops lemon juice
10ml/2 tsp chopped fresh parsley or
   thyme
¼ red pepper, seeded and chopped
salt and black pepper
fresh basil leaves, to garnish

1 To make the popovers, whisk the egg and flour together and gradually add a little milk to blend, then whisk in the rest of the milk to make a smooth batter. Add a pinch of salt and leave the batter to stand for 10–20 minutes.

2 When required, preheat the oven to 190°C/425°F/Gas 7. Pour very little oil into the base of eight Yorkshire pudding tins and heat through in the oven for 4–5 minutes. Pour the batter into the very hot tins and cook for 20 minutes or until well risen and crispy.

3 Meanwhile, make the filling; heat the oil and sauté the mushrooms with the lemon juice, herbs and seasoning until most of their liquid has evaporated. Add the red pepper at the last minute so that it keeps its crunch. Season to taste.

4 To serve, spoon the filling into the hot popover cases and scatter over the basil leaves.

NUTTY DEVILLED EGGS

INGREDIENTS

Serves 6

9 hard-boiled eggs
50g/2oz/¼ cup finely chopped
    cooked ham
6 walnut halves, very finely chopped
15ml/1 tbsp very finely chopped
    spring onion
15ml/1 tbsp Dijon mustard
15ml/1 tbsp mayonnaise
10ml/2 tsp white wine vinegar
1.25ml/¼ tsp cayenne pepper
salt and black pepper
paprika and a few slices of dill pickle,
    to garnish

1 Cut each egg in half lengthways. Place the yolks in a bowl and set the whites aside.

2 Mash the yolks well with a fork, or push them through a sieve. Add all the remaining ingredients and mix well with the yolks. Season to taste with salt, pepper and cayenne.

3 Spoon the filling into the egg white halves, or pipe it in with a piping bag fitted with a wide nozzle. Sprinkle the top of each stuffed egg with a little paprika and garnish with a small piece of dill pickle. Serve the stuffed eggs at room temperature.

STUFFED CELERY STICKS

INGREDIENTS

Serves 4–6

12 celery sticks
25g/1oz/¼ cup crumbled blue cheese
115g/4oz/½ cup cream cheese
45ml/3 tbsp soured cream
50g/2oz/½ cup chopped walnuts

2 Place the crumbled blue cheese, cream cheese and soured cream in a small bowl. Stir together with a wooden spoon until smoothly blended. Fold in all but 15ml/1 tbsp of the chopped walnuts.

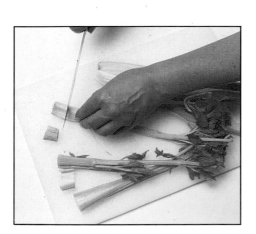

1 Cut the celery into 10cm/4in pieces. Reserve the leaves.

3 Fill the celery with the cheese mixture. Chill, then garnish with the reserved walnuts and celery leaves.

VARIATION
You could use the same filling to stuff scooped-out cherry tomatoes.

LEEKS WITH MUSTARD DRESSING

Pencil-slim baby leeks are increasingly available nowadays, and are beautifully tender. Use three or four of these smaller leeks per serving.

INGREDIENTS

Serves 4

8 slim leeks, each about 13cm/5in long
5–10ml/1–2 tsp Dijon mustard
10ml/2 tsp white wine vinegar
1 hard-boiled egg, halved lengthways
75ml/5 tbsp light olive oil
10ml/2 tsp chopped fresh parsley
salt and pepper

1 Steam the leeks over a pan of boiling water until just tender.

2 Meanwhile, stir together the mustard and vinegar in a bowl. Scoop the egg yolk into the bowl and mash thoroughly into the vinegar mixture using a fork.

3 Gradually work in the oil to make a smooth sauce, then season to taste.

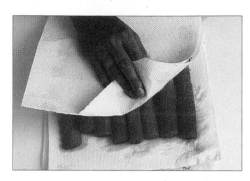

4 Lift the leeks out of the steamer and place on several layers of kitchen paper, then cover the leeks with several more layers of kitchen paper and pat dry.

5 Transfer the leeks to a serving dish while still warm, spoon the dressing over them and leave to cool. Finely chop the egg white using a large sharp knife, then mix with the chopped fresh parsley and scatter over the leeks. Chill until ready to serve.

COOK'S TIP
Although this dish is served cold, make sure that the leeks are still warm when you pour over the dressing so that they will absorb the mustardy flavours.

STUFFED MUSHROOMS

INGREDIENTS

Serves 4
275g/10oz spinach, stalks removed
400g/14oz medium cap mushrooms
25g/1oz/2 tbsp butter, plus extra for
  brushing
25g/1oz bacon, chopped
½ small onion, finely chopped
75ml/5 tbsp double (heavy) cream
about 60ml/4 tbsp finely grated
  Cheddar cheese
2 tbsp fresh breadcrumbs
salt and pepper
sprig of parsley, to garnish

1 Preheat the oven to 190°C/375°F/
Gas 5. Butter a baking dish. Wash
but do not dry the spinach. Place it in
a pan and cook, stirring occasionally,
until wilted and no liquid is visible.

2 Tip the spinach into a colander and
squeeze out as much liquid as
possible. Chop finely. Snap the stalks
from the mushrooms and chop the
stalks finely.

3 Melt the butter, then cook the
bacon, onion and mushroom stalks
for about 5 minutes. Stir in the
spinach, cook for a moment or two,
then remove the pan from the heat and
stir in the cream and seasoning.

4 Brush the mushroom caps with
melted butter, then place, gills
uppermost, in a single layer in the
baking dish.

5 Divide the spinach mixture among
the mushrooms. Mix together the
cheese and breadcrumbs, sprinkle over
the mushrooms, then bake for about
20 minutes, until the mushrooms are
tender. Serve warm, garnished with a
sprig of parsley.

WATCHPOINT
It is important to make sure that
all the surplus liquid is squeezed
out of the spinach, otherwise the
stuffing will be too soggy.

EGGY BREAD WITH CHEESE

Although very simple – or perhaps because of its simplicity – Eggy Bread has been popular for generations, and is enjoyed by all age groups.

───── INGREDIENTS ─────

Serves 2 – 4
3 eggs
75ml/5 tbsp milk
45ml/3 tbsp chopped fresh herbs such as tarragon, parsley and chervil
4 slices bread
4 slices Red Leicester cheese
40g/1½oz/3 tbsp butter
salt and pepper

1 Lightly beat the eggs, milk, herbs and seasoning together. Pour into a large shallow dish.

2 Cut the crusts from the bread and make into sandwiches with the cheese. Cut them in half to make triangles, then dip both sides of each sandwich in the milk mixture.

3 Heat the butter in a frying pan, add the bread and fry until golden on both sides. Serve at once.

SAVOURY SCRAMBLED EGGS

Known as 'Scotch Woodcock', these eggs were popular in Victorian and Edwardian times as a savoury served instead of cheese at the end of a meal.

───── INGREDIENTS ─────

Serves 2
2 slices bread
40g/1½oz/3 tbsp butter, plus extra for spreading
anchovy paste such as Gentleman's Relish
2 eggs, beaten
2 egg yolks
60–90ml/4–6 tbsp cream or milk
salt and pepper
anchovy fillets cut into strips, and paprika for garnish

1 Toast the bread, spread with butter and anchovy paste, then remove the crusts and cut into fingers. Keep warm, while you make the scrambled eggs.

2 Melt the rest of the butter in a non-stick saucepan, then stir in the eggs, egg yolks, cream or milk, a little salt, and pepper. Heat very gently, stirring constantly, until the mixture begins to thicken.

3 Remove the pan from the heat and continue to stir until the mixture becomes creamy.

4 Spoon the egg mixture evenly on to the toast fingers and garnish with strips of anchovy fillet and a sprinkling of paprika. Serve immediately.

WELSH RABBIT

This delicious supper dish is made from toast and a flavourful cheese sauce. It doesn't, as the name might suggest, contain any meat. It is sometimes called 'Welsh rarebit', although 'rabbit' seems to have been the original name. To turn Welsh Rabbit into Buck Rabbit, top each portion with a poached egg.

─── INGREDIENTS ───

Serves 4
4 thick slices of bread, crusts removed
25g/1oz/2 tbsp butter
225g/8oz/2 cups grated mature
  Cheddar cheese
5ml/1 tsp English mustard powder
few drops Worcestershire sauce
60ml/4 tbsp brown ale, beer or milk

1 Preheat the grill (broiler). Toast the bread until golden, then place in a single layer in a wide, shallow baking dish. Keep warm.

2 Melt the butter in a small to medium, heavy-based, preferably non-stick saucepan over a very low heat, or in a bowl placed over a saucepan of hot water.

3 Stir the grated Cheddar cheese, English mustard powder and Worcestershire sauce into the melted butter, then slowly pour in the ale, beer or milk in a steady stream, stirring the cheese mixture all the time until very well blended.

┌─────────────────────────────┐
│ COOK'S TIP   │
│ Use a strong flavoured cheese so │
│ the topping has plenty of flavour. │
└─────────────────────────────┘

4 Spoon the cheese mixture onto the toast then place under the hot grill (broiler) until bubbling and golden. Serve immediately.

DEVILLED KIDNEYS

'Devilled' dishes are always hot and spicy. If you have time, mix the spicy ingredients together in advance to give the flavours time to mingle and mature.

INGREDIENTS

Serves 4

10ml/2 tsp Worcestershire sauce
15ml/1 tbsp prepared English mustard
15ml/1 tbsp lemon juice
15ml/1 tbsp tomato purée (paste)
pinch of cayenne pepper
40g/1½ oz/3 tbsp butter
1 shallot, finely chopped
8 lambs' kidneys, skinned, halved and cored
salt and pepper
15ml/1 tbsp chopped fresh parsley, to garnish

1 Mix the Worcestershire sauce, mustard, lemon juice, tomato purée (paste), cayenne pepper and salt together to make a sauce.

2 Melt the butter in a frying pan, add the shallot and cook, stirring occasionally, until softened but not coloured.

COOK'S TIP
To remove the cores from the kidneys, use kitchen scissors, rather than a knife – you will find that it is much easier.

3 Stir the kidney halves into the shallot in the pan and cook over a medium–high heat for about 3 minutes on each side.

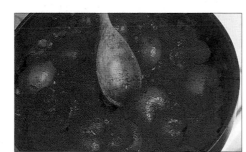

4 Pour the sauce over the kidneys and quickly stir so they are evenly coated. Serve immediately, sprinkled with chopped parsley.

TUNA FISHCAKE BITES

An updated version of a traditional British tea-time dish.

INGREDIENTS

Serves 4

675g/1½lb (about 5 medium) potatoes
knob of butter
2 hard-boiled eggs, chopped
3 spring onions, finely chopped
finely grated rind of ½ lemon
5ml/1 tsp lemon juice
30ml/2 tbsp chopped fresh parsley
200g/7oz can tuna in oil, drained
10ml/2 tsp capers, chopped
2 eggs, lightly beaten
115g/4oz/2 cups fresh white breadcrumbs, for coating
sunflower oil, for frying
salt and black pepper
mixed salad, to serve

For the tartare sauce

60ml/4 tbsp mayonnaise
15ml/1 tbsp natural yogurt
15ml/1 tbsp finely chopped gherkins
15ml/1 tbsp capers, chopped
15ml/1 tbsp chopped fresh parsley

1 Cook the potatoes in a pan of boiling salted water until tender. Drain well, add the butter and mash well. Leave to cool.

2 Add the hard-boiled eggs, spring onions, lemon rind, lemon juice, parsley, tuna, capers and 15ml/1 tbsp of the beaten egg to the cooled potato. Mix well with a fork and season. Cover and chill for about 30 minutes.

3 Meanwhile, place all the ingredients for the tartare sauce in a bowl and mix well. Chill and reserve.

4 Pour the remaining beaten egg into one shallow bowl and the breadcrumbs into another. Roll the chilled fishcake mixture into about 24 balls. Dip these into the egg and then roll gently in the breadcrumbs until evenly coated. Transfer to a plate.

5 Heat 90ml/6 tbsp of oil in a frying pan and fry the balls on a moderate heat, in batches, for about 4 minutes, turning two or three times until browned all over. Drain on kitchen paper and keep warm in the oven while frying the remainder.

6 Serve about six balls per person with the tartare sauce and a salad.

CRUMB-COATED PRAWNS

INGREDIENTS

Serves 4
90g/3½oz/¾ cup polenta
about 5–10ml/1–2 tsp cayenne
  pepper
2.5ml/½ tsp ground cumin
5ml/1 tsp salt
30ml/2 tbsp chopped fresh coriander
  or parsley
1kg/2lb raw large prawns, peeled and
  deveined
plain flour, for dredging
45ml/3 tbsp/¼ cup vegetable oil
115g/4oz/1 cup coarsely grated
  Cheddar cheese
lime wedges and fresh tomato salsa,
  to serve

1 Preheat the grill. Mix the polenta, cayenne pepper, cumin, salt and coriander or parsley in a bowl.

2 Coat the prawns lightly in flour, then dip them in water and roll in the polenta mixture to coat evenly.

3 Heat the oil in a frying pan. When hot, add the prawns, in batches if necessary. Cook for 2–3 minutes on each side, until they are cooked through. Drain on kitchen paper.

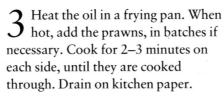

4 Place the prawns in a large baking dish, or in four individual flameproof dishes. Sprinkle the cheese evenly over the top. Grill for 2–3 minutes, until the cheese melts. Serve immediately, with lime wedges and the tomato salsa.

CRAB SAVOURY

INGREDIENTS

Serves 4

25g/1oz/2 tbsp butter
1 small onion, finely chopped
50g/2oz/1 firmly packed cup fresh
   brown breadcrumbs
225g/8oz crabmeat
150ml/¼pt/⅔ cup soured
   (sour) cream
10–15ml/2–3tsp prepared mustard
pinch of cayenne pepper
squeeze of lemon juice
75ml/5 tbsp finely grated
   Cheddar cheese
salt

1 Melt the butter in a saucepan, then cook the onion gently until soft but not brown. Meanwhile, preheat the grill (broiler).

2 Stir the breadcrumbs, crabmeat, soured (sour) cream and mustard into the onions. Add a generous sprinkling of cayenne pepper, lemon juice and salt to taste. Heat through gently, stirring carefully.

3 Spoon the crab mixture into a baking dish, sprinkle the cheese over the top and place under the hot grill (broiler) until golden and bubbling.

SMOKED MACKEREL PÂTÉ

The pâté can be flavoured with horseradish, if liked.

INGREDIENTS

Serves 4

275g/10oz smoked mackerel fillet,
   skinned
90ml/6 tbsp soured (sour) cream
75g/3oz/6 tbsp unsalted (sweet) butter,
   softened
30ml/2 tbsp chopped fresh parsley
15–30 ml/1–2 tbsp lemon juice
pepper
chicory leaves and parsley, to garnish
fingers of toast, to serve

> **COOK'S TIP**
> For a less rich (and lower calorie) version of this pâté, substitute 200g/7oz/scant 1 cup low fat soft cheese or sieved cottage cheese for the soured (sour) cream.

1 Remove any bones from the mackerel, then mash it using a fork.

2 Work the soured (sour) cream and butter into the mackerel until smooth. Stir in the parsley, and add lemon juice and pepper to taste.

3 Pack the mackerel mixture into a dish or bowl, then cover tightly and chill overnight.

4 About 30 minutes before serving, remove the pâté from the fridge to allow it to return to room temperature. To serve, spoon on to individual plates and garnish with chicory leaves and parsley. Serve with fingers of toast.

MUSSELS IN BACON

This recipe is based on the well-known 'angels on horseback' in which oysters are wrapped in bacon, then served on squares of toast.

INGREDIENTS

Serves 4
16 cooked and shelled mussels
juice of 1 lemon
about 30ml/2 tbsp Worcestershire
   sauce
few drops Tabasco sauce
8 slices streaky bacon
lemon wedges and toast or bread,
   to serve

1 Place the mussels in a bowl with the lemon juice, Worcestershire sauce and Tabasco sauce, lightly toss the mussels, then cover and leave in a cool place for 30 minutes.

2 Meanwhile, stretch each slice of bacon with the back of a knife, then cut each slice across in half.

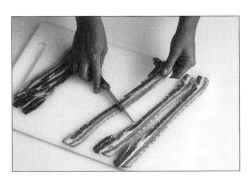

3 Preheat the grill (broiler). Remove the mussels from the bowl, then wrap a piece of bacon around each one. Secure each wrapped mussel with a wooden cocktail stick (toothpick).

4 Place the wrapped mussels on a grill rack and cook under the grill (broiler) for 3–5 minutes, until the bacon is crisp, turning frequently. Remove the cocktail sticks (toothpicks) before serving with lemon wedges and toast or bread.

GLAMORGAN SAUSAGES

These tasty sausages are ideal for vegetarians as they are made from cheese and leeks rather than meat.

INGREDIENTS

Makes 8
150g/5oz/2½ cups fresh breadcrumbs
150g/5oz generous cup grated
   Caerphilly cheese
1 small leek, very finely chopped
15ml/1 tbsp chopped fresh parsley
leaves from 1 thyme sprig, chopped
2 eggs
7.5ml/1½ tsp English mustard
   powder
about 45ml/3 tbsp milk
plain (all-purpose) flour, for coating
15ml/1 tbsp oil
15g/½oz/1 tbsp butter, melted
salt and pepper

1 Mix the breadcrumbs, cheese, leek, herbs and seasoning. Whisk the eggs with the mustard and reserve 30ml/2 tbsp. Stir the rest into the cheese mixture with enough milk to bind.

2 Divide the cheese mixture into eight and form into sausage shapes.

3 Dip the sausages in the reserved egg to coat. Season the flour, then roll the sausages in it to give a light, even coating. Chill for about 30 minutes until firm.

4 Preheat the grill (broiler) and oil the grill rack. Mix the oil and melted butter together and brush over the sausages. Grill (broil) the sausages for 5–10 minutes, turning carefully occasionally, until golden brown all over. Serve hot or cold.

SAVOURY DISHES

Many dishes that are now popular as supper or lunch dishes, such as Macaroni Cheese and Toad In The Hole, were served at high tea. This meal was eaten at about 6 o'clock and consisted of a savoury dish, usually accompanied by bread and butter, and cake. Other dishes, such as Bacon And Egg Pie and Cornish Pasties, made handy 'edible packages' for farmers and miners respectively, to take into the fields and down the mines for their lunch. Traditional vegetable dishes, often regional and frequently sources of simple, inexpensive meals for the poor, such as Pan Haggerty, also now provide us with the basis of a quick lunch or supper. Many savoury dishes are ideal for vegetarians.

Monday Savoury Omelette

Here is a very tasty way to use up leftover meat, vegetables, rice, or pasta from the weekend.

Ingredients

Serves 4–6

30ml/2 tbsp olive oil
1 large onion, chopped
2 large garlic cloves, crushed
115g/4oz bacon, rinds removed, and chopped
50g/2oz cold cooked meat, chopped
115g/4oz leftover cooked vegetables (preferably ones which are not too soft)
115g/4oz leftover cooked rice or pasta
4 eggs
30ml/2 tbsp chopped, mixed fresh herbs, such as parsley, chives, marjoram or tarragon, or 10ml/2 tsp dried
5ml/1 tsp Worcestershire sauce, or more to taste
15ml/1 tbsp grated mature Cheddar cheese
salt and black pepper

1 Heat the oil in a large flameproof frying pan and sauté the onion, garlic and bacon until all the fat has run out of the bacon.

2 Add the chopped meat, vegetables and rice. Beat the eggs, herbs and Worcestershire sauce together with seasoning. Pour over the rice or pasta and vegetables, stir slightly, then leave the omelette mixture undisturbed to cook gently for about 5 minutes.

3 When beginning to set, sprinkle with cheese and place under the grill until just firm and golden.

COOK'S TIP
This is surprisingly good cold, so is perfect for taking on picnics, or using for packed lunches.

FISH SOUFFLÉ WITH CHEESE TOPPING

This is an easy-going soufflé, which will not drop too much if kept waiting. On the other hand, it might be best to get the family seated before you take it out of the oven!

INGREDIENTS

Serves 4

350g/12oz white fish, skinned and
  boned
150ml/¼ pint/⅔ cup milk
225g/8oz cooked potatoes, still warm
1 garlic clove, crushed
2 eggs, separated
grated rind and juice of ½ small lemon
115g/4oz/1 cup cooked, peeled prawns
50g/2oz/½ cup grated Cheddar cheese
salt and black pepper

1 Poach, or microwave, the fish in the milk until it flakes easily. Drain, reserving the milk, and place the fish in a bowl.

2 Mash the potatoes until really creamy, using as much of the fish milk as necessary. Then mash in the garlic, egg yolks, lemon rind and juice and seasoning to taste.

3 Preheat the oven to 220°C/425°F/ Gas 7. Flake the fish and gently stir into the potato mixture with the prawns. Season to taste.

4 Whisk the egg whites until stiff but not dry and gently fold them into the fish mixture. When smoothly blended, spoon into a greased gratin dish.

5 Sprinkle with the cheese and bake for 25–30 minutes, until the top is golden and just about firm to the touch. (If it browns too quickly, turn the temperature down to 200°C/400°F/Gas 6.)

> **COOK'S TIP**
> Smoked fish is also good for this soufflé, but as it has a stronger flavour, you could use less lemon and cheese.

KEDGEREE

Popular for breakfast in Victorian times, Kedgeree has its origins in Khichri, an Indian rice and lentil dish, and is often flavoured with curry powder.

INGREDIENTS

Serves 4

500g/1¼ lb smoked haddock
115g/4oz/generous ½ cup long grain rice
30ml/2 tbsp lemon juice
150ml/5 fl oz/⅔ cup single (light) or soured (sour) cream
pinch of freshly grated nutmeg
pinch of cayenne pepper
2 hard-boiled eggs, peeled and cut into wedges
50g/2oz/4 tbsp butter, diced
30ml/2 tbsp chopped fresh parsley
salt and pepper
parsley sprigs, to garnish

1 Poach the haddock, just covered by water, for about 10 minutes, until the flesh flakes easily. Lift the fish from the cooking liquid using a slotted spoon, then remove any skin and bones flake the flesh.

2 Pour the rice into a measuring jug and note the volume, then tip out, pour the fish cooking liquid into the jug and top up with water, until it measures twice the volume of the rice.

3 Bring the fish cooking liquid to the boil, add the rice, stir, then cover and simmer for about 15 minutes, until the rice is tender and the liquid absorbed. While the rice is cooking, preheat the oven to 180°C/350°F/ Gas 4, and butter a baking dish.

4 Remove the rice from the heat and stir in the lemon juice, cream, flaked fish, nutmeg and cayenne. Add the egg wedges to the rice mixture and stir in gently.

5 Tip the rice mixture into the baking dish, dot with butter and bake for about 25 minutes.

6 Stir the chopped parsley into the Kedgeree, check the seasoning and garnish with parsley sprigs.

COOK'S TIP
Taste the Kedgeree before you add salt, since the smoked haddock may already be quite salty.

BUBBLE AND SQUEAK

The name is derived from the bubbling of the vegetables as they boiled for their first cooking, and the way they squeak when they are fried.

INGREDIENTS

60ml/4 tbsp dripping, bacon fat or oil
1 onion, finely chopped
450g/1 lb potatoes, cooked and
mashed
225g/8oz cooked cabbage or Brussels
sprouts, finely chopped
salt and pepper

1 Heat half the dripping, fat or oil in a heavy frying pan. Add the onion and cook, stirring frequently, until softened, but not browned.

2 Mix together the potatoes, cabbage or sprouts and season to taste with salt and plenty of pepper.

3 Add the vegetables to the pan, stir well, then press the vegetable mixture into a large, even cake.

4 Cook over a moderate heat for about 15 minutes, until the cake is browned underneath.

5 Hold a large plate over the pan, then invert the vegetable cake on to it. Add the remaining fat or oil to the pan, then, when hot, slip the cake back into the pan, browned side uppermost.

6 Cook the Bubble and Squeak over a moderate heat for a further 10 minutes or so, until the underside of the cake is golden brown, then serve hot, cut into wedges.

COOK'S TIP
If you don't have left-over, cooked cabbage or brussels sprouts, use fresh raw vegetables instead. Shred the cabbage first and cook both in boiling salted water until just tender. Drain thoroughly, then chop and continue from step 2.

Macaroni Cheese with Leeks

Leeks add a new twist and extra flavour to an ever-popular family favourite.

Ingredients

Serves 4
175g/6oz/1½ cups short-cut macaroni
50g/2oz/4 tbsp butter
4 leeks, chopped
60ml/5 tbsp plain (all-purpose) flour
750ml/1¼ pints/3 cups milk
200g/7oz/scant 2 cups grated mature Cheddar cheese
45ml/3 tbsp fresh breadcrumbs
salt and pepper

> **Cook's Tip**
> The sauce can be flavoured with mustard or chopped herbs, such as parsley, chives or thyme.

1 Preheat the oven to 200°C/400°F/ Gas 6. Cook the macaroni in plenty of boiling salted water for 8–10 minutes, until tender. Drain well.

2 Melt the butter in a saucepan, add the leeks and cook, stirring occasionally, for about 4 minutes. Stir in the flour, cook for 1 minute, then remove the pan from the heat.

3 Gradually stir the milk into the pan, then return to the heat and bring to the boil, stirring. Simmer for about 3 minutes.

4 Remove from the heat and stir in the macaroni and most of the cheese, and season to taste. Pour the macaroni mixture into a baking dish. Mix together the breadcrumbs and the remaining cheese, then sprinkle over the dish. Bake for 20–25 minutes, until the topping is golden.

Broccoli and Stilton Puff

Cauliflower can be used instead of broccoli in this dish, or if you like, you can use a mixture of the two.

Ingredients

Serves 4
675g/1½ lb broccoli
4 eggs, separated
115g/4oz blue Stilton cheese, crumbled
about 10ml/2 tsp wholegrain or French mustard
salt and pepper

1 Preheat the oven to 190°C/375°F/ Gas 5. Thoroughly butter a 19cm/7½ in soufflé dish.

2 Cook the broccoli in boiling salted water until just tender. Drain the broccoli, refresh under cold running water, then drain well.

3 Place the broccoli in a food processor with the egg yolks and process until smooth. Tip the mixture into a bowl then mix in the Stilton and add mustard and seasoning to taste.

4 Whisk the egg whites until stiff but not dry, then gently fold into the broccoli mixture in three batches. Transfer the broccoli mixture to the dish and bake for about 35 minutes, until risen, just set in the centre, and golden. Serve immediately.

EASY HAM LOAF

INGREDIENTS

Serves 8–10

675g/1½ lb lean unsmoked gammon or
*   boiling bacon*
1 onion, quartered
2 large garlic cloves
350g/12oz sausagemeat
175g/6oz/3 cups fresh breadcrumbs
30ml/2 tbsp chopped, mixed fresh
*   herbs, or 10ml/2 tsp dried*
10ml/2 tsp grated orange rind
1 egg
salt and black pepper

For the sauce

4 tomatoes, peeled, seeded and chopped
1 shallot, chopped
60ml/4 tbsp fresh orange juice
10ml/2 tsp balsamic or sherry vinegar
10ml/2 tsp olive oil
15ml/1 tbsp chopped fresh basil
few basil leaves, to garnish

1 Preheat the oven to 180°C/350°F/ Gas 4. Finely chop the gammon, onion and garlic in a food processor, then mix in the rest of the ingredients until well blended. Season to taste.

2 Pack into a 900g/2 lb loaf tin. Cover with greaseproof paper and bake for 1½ hours, or until firm.

3 Meanwhile, make the sauce; simmer the tomatoes, shallot, orange juice, vinegar, olive oil, chopped fresh basil for 10–12 minutes, stirring occasionally. Add seasoning, to taste.

4 Serve the ham loaf hot or cold, with the tomato sauce, and accompanied by new potatoes and broccoli.

LAMBURGERS WITH MELTING CENTRES

Try these lamb-based hamburgers on the children, for a change, but keep them quite small. You can prepare them in advance and freeze them, between sheets of greaseproof paper.

INGREDIENTS

Makes 6

450g/1 lb minced lamb
few drops Worcestershire sauce
pinch dried marjoram
50g/2oz Bel Paese, feta or other tasty,
*   but not strong cheese, diced*
salt and black pepper
little olive oil

1 Place the minced lamb in a bowl with the Worcestershire sauce, marjoram, and seasoning to taste and mix thoroughly.

2 Divide the mixture into six and push a little of the diced cheese into the middle of each one. Mould the lamb around the cheese, shape into hamburgers and leave to stand for 10–20 minutes.

3 Brush the grill pan and the burgers lightly with oil and grill under a high heat, for 3–5 minutes on each side, or until cooked to your liking.

4 Serve the lamburgers with Italian ciabatta bread and a salad.

TOAD IN THE HOLE

Sausages are cooked in a light batter which rises to a crisp, brown crust, making this a tasty and substantial supper dish.

INGREDIENTS

Serves 4

90g/3½oz/scant 1 cup plain
  (all-purpose) flour
30ml/2 tbsp chopped fresh parsley
10ml/2 tsp chopped fresh thyme
1 egg, beaten
300ml/½ pint/1¼ cups milk and water,
  mixed
60ml/4 tbsp oil
450g/1 lb good-quality sausages
salt

1 Stir the flour, herbs and salt together in a bowl and form a well in the centre.

2 Pour the egg into the well, then gradually pour in the milk and water while stirring the dry ingredients into the liquids. Beat to form a smooth batter, then leave for 30 minutes.

3 Preheat the oven to 220°C/425°F/ Gas 7. Pour the oil into a small roasting tin (pan) or baking dish, add the sausages, turn them to coat them thoroughly in the oil, then cook the sausages in the oven for 10–15 minutes, until they are beginning to brown all over and the oil is very hot.

4 Stir the batter using a wooden spoon, then remove the roasting tin (pan) or baking dish from the oven and quickly pour the batter over the sausages and return the roasting tin (pan) or baking dish to the oven to bake for about 40 minutes (depending on the depth of the batter), until well risen and crisp around the edges.

COOK'S TIP
It is important to preheat the oil with the sausages so that the batter rises well and becomes crisp.

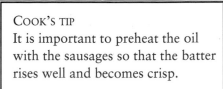

CORNISH PASTIES

There are many traditional recipes for pasties, which were the original packed lunch, but usually people just used to add whatever was available.

INGREDIENTS

Makes 6
500–675g/1¼–1½lb ready-made
  shortcrust (pie) pastry
450g/1lb chuck steak, diced
1 potato, about 175g/6oz, diced
175g/6oz swede (rutabaga), diced
1 onion, chopped
2.5ml/½ tsp dried mixed herbs
a little beaten egg, to glaze
salt and pepper

1 Preheat the oven to 220°C/425°F/ Gas 7. Divide the pastry into six equal pieces, then roll out each piece to a 20cm/8 in round.

2 Mix together the steak, vegetables, herbs and seasoning, then spoon an equal amount on to one half of each pastry round.

COOK'S TIP
Other vegetables, such as turnip, carrot or celery could be used in place of the swede (rutabaga), if you prefer.

3 Brush the pastry edges with water, then fold the free half of each round over the filling. Press the edges firmly together to seal.

4 Use a fish slice to transfer the pasties to a baking (cookie) sheet, then brush each one with beaten egg.

5 Bake the pasties for 15 minutes, then reduce the oven temperature to 160°C/325°F/Gas 3 and bake for a further hour. Serve hot or cold.

Cheese-Filled Baked Onions

Serve with roast or grilled (broiled) meats, or for a light meal accompanied by a crisp salad and crusty wholemeal or Granary bread.

INGREDIENTS

Serves 4
4 large onions
115g/4oz/1 cup grated mature
  Cheddar cheese
15ml/1 tbsp chopped fresh parsley
40g/1½oz/3 tbsp butter, melted
salt and pepper

1 Peel the onions, then cook in boiling salted water for 15 minutes.

2 Preheat the oven to 180°C/350°F/Gas 4. Drain the onions, rinse under cold running water, then drain again and cut off the top from each onion using a sharp knife.

3 Carefully remove the central layers of each onion. Finely chop the scooped-out onion and the onion tops, mix with the cheese, parsley and seasoning, then pile back into the onions.

COOK'S TIP
Substitute another strong flavoured cheese such as blue Stilton, farmhouse Lancashire, or red or blue Cheshire for the mature Cheddar, if you like.

4 Place the onions in a baking dish, spoon over the butter and bake for about 30 minutes, basting occasionally, until tender.

MACARONI AND BLUE CHEESE

── INGREDIENTS ──

Serves 6
450g/1lb macaroni
1.2 litres/2 pints/5 cups milk
50g/2oz/4 tbsp butter
75g/3oz plain flour
*225g/8oz blue Stilton cheese,
  crumbled*
salt and black pepper

1 Preheat the oven to 180°C/350°F/
Gas 4. Grease a shallow
33 × 23cm/13 × 9in ovenproof dish.

2 Bring a large pan of salted water to
the boil. Add the macaroni and
cook for 10–12 minutes, until just
tender. Drain the macaroni and rinse
under cold running water. Place in a
large bowl. Set aside.

3 In another pan, bring the milk to
the boil and set aside.

4 Melt the butter in a heavy-based
saucepan over a low heat. Whisk in
the flour and cook for 1–2 minutes,
whisking constantly and taking care not
to let the mixture brown.

5 Remove the pan from the heat and
whisk the hot milk into the butter
and flour mixture. When the mixture is
smoothly blended, return to a medium
heat and continue cooking, whisking
constantly for about 5 minutes, until
the sauce is thick. Season to taste.

6 Stir the sauce into the macaroni.
Add three-quarters of the crumbled
blue cheese and stir well. Transfer the
macaroni mixture to the prepared
ovenproof dish and spread evenly.

7 Sprinkle the remaining cheese
evenly over the surface. Bake for
about 25 minutes, until the macaroni is
bubbling hot.

8 Preheat the grill and lightly brown
the top of the macaroni and cheese.
Serve immediately, sprinkled with extra
freshly ground black pepper, if you like.

SAVOURY POTATO CAKES

Serve hot on their own with a salad, and a dollop of soured (sour) cream, plain yogurt or tomato sauce, if you like.

INGREDIENTS

Serves 4
450g/1 lb potatoes, grated
1 small onion, grated
2 slices streaky bacon, finely chopped
30ml/2 tbsp self-raising (self-rising) flour
2 eggs, beaten
oil, for frying
salt and pepper

1 Rinse the potatoes, drain and pat dry, then mix with the onion, bacon, flour, eggs and seasoning.

2 Heat a 1cm/½ in layer of oil in a frying pan (skillet), then add about 15ml/1 tbsp of the potato mixture and quickly spread the mixture out with the back of the spoon.

3 Add a few more spoonfuls of the mixture in the same way, leaving space between each one, and cook for 4–5 minutes, until golden underneath.

4 Turn the cakes over and cook for 3–4 minutes until the other side is golden brown. Lift the potato cakes out of the pan and transfer to a heated serving dish and keep warm while frying the remaining potato mixture in the same way.

PAN HAGGERTY

Serve this Northumberland dish cut into wedges for a snack, supper or light lunch, accompanied by a crisp salad.

INGREDIENTS

Serves 4
60ml/4 tbsp oil
450g/1 lb firm potatoes, thinly sliced
1 large onion, thinly sliced
115g/4oz/1 cup grated mature Cheddar cheese
salt and pepper

> **COOK'S TIP**
> Use any well flavoured hard cheese, in place of the Cheddar.

1 Heat the oil in a large, heavy frying pan. Remove the pan from the heat and arrange alternate layers of potato, onion and cheese, starting and ending with a layer of potatoes, and seasoning each layer.

2 Cook for 30 minutes, starting over a low heat and then increasing it so the underside of the mixture browns. Meanwhile, preheat the grill (broiler).

3 Place the pan under the grill (broiler) for 5–10 minutes to brown the top of the Pan Haggerty. Slide the Pan Haggerty on to a warm plate and cut into wedges.

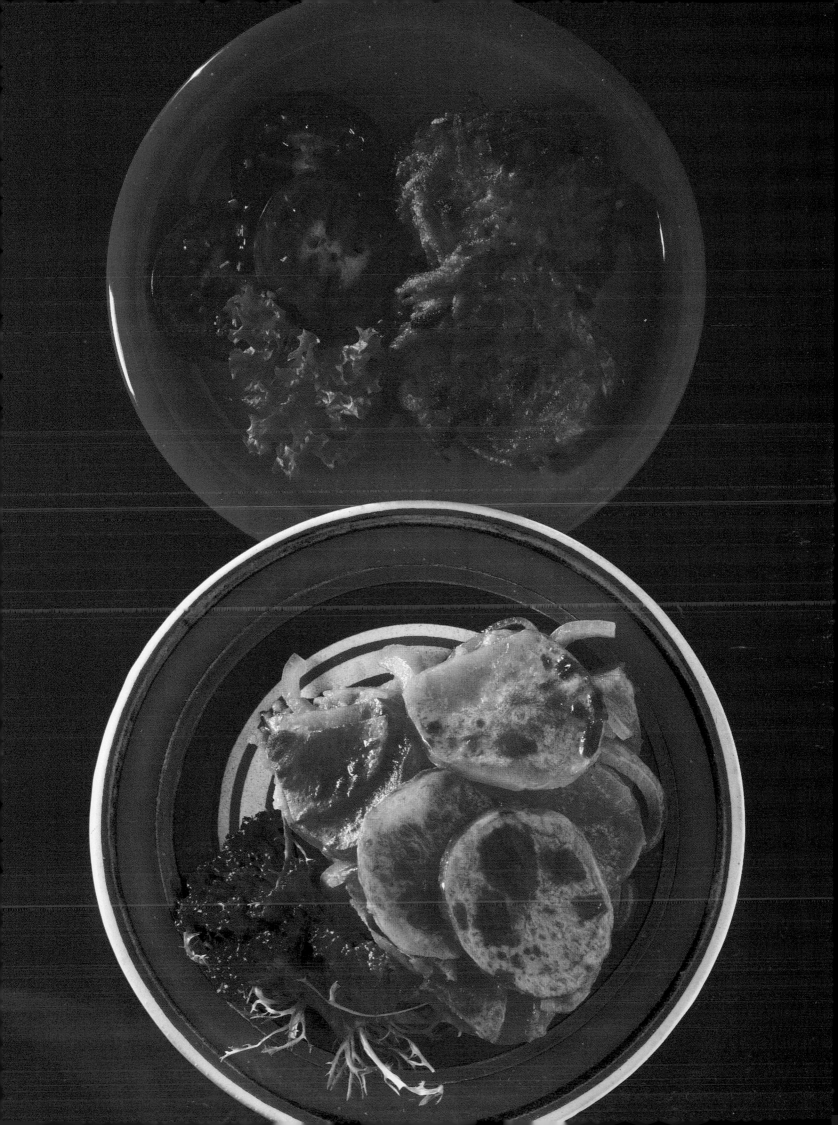

Eggs With Spinach And Cheese Sauce

If fresh spinach is not available, thaw 450g/1 lb frozen spinach and squeeze it hard to expel surplus liquid; use in the recipe from step 4.

INGREDIENTS

Serves 4

1kg/2 lb fresh spinach, stalks removed
40g/1½oz/3 tbsp butter or margarine
45ml/3 tbsp plain (all-purpose) flour
300ml/½ pint/1¼ cups milk
75g/3oz/¾ cup grated mature Cheddar
 cheese
pinch of English mustard powder
large pinch of freshly grated nutmeg
4 hard-boiled eggs, peeled and halved
 lengthways
salt and pepper

1 Wash but do not dry the spinach, then place in a large saucepan with just the water clinging to the leaves. Cook until the spinach is wilted and no free liquid is visible. Tip the spinach into a sieve (strainer) and squeeze out as much liquid as possible, then chop.

2 Melt 25g/1oz/2 tbsp of the butter or margarine in a saucepan, stir in the flour, cook for 1 minute, then remove from the heat. Gradually add the milk, stirring constantly, then return to the heat and bring to the boil, stirring. Simmer gently for about 4 minutes.

3 Remove from the heat and stir in 50g/2oz/4 tbsp cheese, the mustard and seasoning. Preheat the grill (broiler).

4 Melt the remaining butter in a small saucepan, then stir in the spinach, nutmeg and seasoning and warm through. Transfer the spinach to a shallow baking dish and arrange the egg halves on top in a single layer.

5 Pour the sauce over the eggs, sprinkle with the remaining cheese and place under the grill (broiler) until golden and bubbling.

BACON AND EGG PIE

INGREDIENTS

Serves 4

450–500g/1–1¼ lb ready-made
shortcrust (pie) pastry
beaten egg or milk, to glaze

For The Filling

30ml/2 tbsp oil
4 slices smoked bacon, cut into 4cm/
1½ in pieces
1 small onion, finely chopped
5 eggs
22.5ml (1½ tbsp) chopped fresh parsley
(optional)
salt and pepper

1 Butter a deep 20cm/8in flan tin (quiche pan). Roll out two-thirds of the pastry on a lightly floured surface and use to line the flan tin (quiche pan). Cover the pastry case and chill for 30 minutes.

2 Preheat the oven to 200°C/400°F/ Gas 6. In a small heavy pan, cook the oil and bacon until the bacon fat begins to run, then add the onion and cook gently until soft. Transfer to kitchen paper to drain and cool.

3 Cover the bottom of the pastry case with the bacon mixture, spreading it evenly, then break the eggs on to the bacon, spacing them evenly apart. Carefully tilt the flan tin (quiche pan) so the egg whites flow together. Sprinkle the eggs with the chopped fresh parsley, if used, plenty of black pepper, and just a little salt if the bacon is very salty. Place a baking (cookie) sheet in the oven to heat.

4 Roll out the remaining pastry, dampen the edges and place over the pie case. Roll over the top with a rolling pin, remove excess pastry and use for pastry leaves. Brush pie with egg and make a hole in the centre.

5 Place the pie on the baking (cookie) sheet and bake for 10 minutes, then reduce the oven temperature to 180°C/ 350°F/Gas 4 and bake for 20 minutes. Leave to cool before cutting.

COOK'S TIP
This pie can be made in a flan ring placed on a baking (cookie) sheet, if preferred.

BAKED EGGS WITH ASPARAGUS

This recipe makes a little asparagus serve six people. If you cook the eggs so the yolks are still soft, they form a delicious sauce for the asparagus and prawns (shrimp).

INGREDIENTS

Serves 6
175g/6oz asparagus
50g/2oz shelled prawns (shrimp), chopped
6 eggs
90ml/6 tbsp whipping (light) cream
30ml/3 tbsp finely grated mature Cheddar Cheese
salt and pepper

1 Preheat the oven to 180°C/350°F/ Gas 4. Butter six 9cm/3½ in ramekin dishes and place in a shallow baking tin (pan).

2 Trim off woody parts from the asparagus, then steam asparagus for 4 minutes, until half cooked.

3 Reserve six tips, chop the remaining asparagus and divide among the ramekins with the prawns (shrimp), then carefully break an egg into each.

4 Season the eggs, then gently spoon 15ml/1 tbsp of cream on to each and lightly spread it out to cover the top completely. Place an asparagus tip on top of each.

5 Sprinkle the cheese over the asparagus and cream, pour boiling water into the baking tin to come halfway up the sides of the dishes, then bake for 12–15 minutes until the eggs are set to the required degree.

EGGS IN BAKED POTATOES

INGREDIENTS

Serves 4
4 large baking potatoes
40g/1½oz/3 tbsp butter
30ml/2 tbsp hot single (light) cream or milk
30ml/2 tbsp snipped fresh chives
4 eggs
about 50g/2oz/½ cup finely grated mature Cheddar cheese
salt and pepper

1 Preheat the oven to 200°F/400°C/ Gas 6. Bake the potatoes for about 1½ hours, until soft.

2 Working quickly, cut a slice about a quarter to a third of the way from the top of each potato, then scoop the flesh into a bowl, taking care not to pierce the potato skins.

3 Add the butter, cream or milk, chives and seasoning to the bowl and mash the ingredients together.

4 Divide the potato mixture between the potato skins, and make a dip in each with the back of a spoon.

5 Break an egg into each dip, season, then return to the oven for about 10 minutes until the eggs are just set. Sprinkle the cheese over the eggs, then place under the grill (broiler) until golden. Serve immediately.

Twice-Baked Cheddar Soufflés

This is an ace of a recipe for busy people and really easy to make. The soufflés can be prepared well in advance, then simply reheated just before serving.

Ingredients

Serves 4

300ml/½ pint/1¼ cups milk
flavouring ingredients (a few onion slices, 1 bay leaf and 4 black peppercorns)
65g/2½oz/5 tbsp butter
40g/1½oz/⅓ cup plain flour
115g/4oz mature Cheddar cheese, grated
1.25ml/¼ tsp mustard powder
3 eggs, separated
20ml/4 tsp chopped fresh parsley
250ml/8fl oz/1 cup double cream
salt and black pepper

1 Preheat the oven to 180°C/350°F/ Gas 4. Put the milk in a pan with the flavouring ingredients. Bring slowly to the boil, then strain into a jug.

> **Cook's Tip**
> Don't attempt to unmould the soufflés until they have cooled, when they will be firmer and easier to handle. They can be kept chilled for up to 8 hours. Use snipped fresh chives instead of the parsley, if you like.

2 Melt the butter in the rinsed-out pan and use a little to grease four 150ml/¼ pint/⅔ cup ramekins.

3 Stir the flour into the remaining butter in the pan and cook for 1 minute. Gradually add the hot milk, then bring to the boil, stirring until thickened and smooth. Cook, stirring all the time, for 2 minutes.

4 Remove the pan from the heat and stir in 75g/3oz of the grated cheese and the mustard powder. Beat in the egg yolks, followed by the chopped parsley, and season to taste with salt and black pepper.

5 Whisk the egg whites in a large bowl until stiff but not dry. Mix in a spoonful of the egg whites to lighten the cheese mixture, then gently fold in the remaining egg whites.

6 Spoon the soufflé mixture into the ramekins, place in a roasting tin and pour in boiling water to come halfway up the sides. Bake the soufflés for 15–20 minutes until risen and set. Remove the ramekins immediately from the roasting tin and allow the soufflés to sink and cool, until ready to serve.

7 When ready to serve, preheat the oven to 220°C/425°F/Gas 7. Carefully turn out the soufflés into a buttered shallow ovenproof dish or individual dishes. Season the cream and pour over the soufflés, then sprinkle over the remaining cheese.

8 Bake the soufflés for about 10–15 minutes, until risen and golden brown. Serve at once.

CAULIFLOWER CHEESE

INGREDIENTS

Serves 4

1 cauliflower, broken into large florets
40g/1½oz/3 tbsp butter
1 small onion, chopped
2 slices streaky bacon, chopped
45ml/3 tbsp plain (all-purpose) flour
450ml/¾ pint/scant 2 cups milk
115g/4oz/1 cup grated mature
  Cheddar cheese
pinch of English mustard powder
salt and pepper

1 Cook the cauliflower in boiling salted water until almost tender. Drain well and tip into a baking dish.

2 Meanwhile, melt the butter in a saucepan and gently cook the onion and bacon until the onion is soft, then spoon over the cauliflower.

3 Stir the flour into the butter in the pan and cook, stirring, for 1 minute. Remove the pan from the heat and slowly pour the milk into the pan, stirring all the time.

4 Return the saucepan to the heat and bring to the boil, stirring constantly. Simmer for 4–5 minutes, stirring occasionally.

5 Preheat the grill (broiler). Remove the pan from the heat and stir in three-quarters of the cheese. Add the mustard and seasoning to taste.

6 Pour the sauce over the cauliflower, sprinkle the remaining cheese over the top and put under the grill (broiler) until the top is golden and bubbling.

GOLDEN CHEESE PUDDING

INGREDIENTS

Serves 4

600ml/1 pint/2½ cups milk
75g/3oz/1¾ cups fresh breadcrumbs
175g/6 oz/1½ cups grated mature
  Cheddar cheese
7.5ml/1½ tsp prepared mustard
4 eggs, separated
salt and pepper

> **COOK'S TIP**
> When whisking egg whites, make sure that both the bowl and beaters are clean and dry.

1 Bring the milk to the boil, then stir in the breadcrumbs.

2 Meanwhile, preheat the oven to 180°C/350°F/Gas 4 and butter a 1.5 litre/2½ pint/6¼ cup baking dish.

3 Whisk the egg whites in a large bowl until stiff but not dry, then carefully fold the egg whites into the breadcrumb mixture using a large spoon or a spatula in three batches.

4 Transfer the mixture to the baking dish and bake for about 30–45 minutes, depending on the depth of the dish, until just lightly set and golden.

MEAT DISHES

There has always been a strong meat-eating tradition in Britain, and at times a family's wealth has been judged by the amount of meat consumed. Britain is famed for her roasts, and well-to-do households would choose large prime-quality joints for Sunday lunch. But there are also dishes developed to deal with cheaper cuts or to 'stretch' meat to make it go further – Lancashire Hotpot and Irish Stew are examples, even Yorkshire Pudding was originally intended to be eaten before the Roast Beef to take the edge off the appetite. There are delicious pastry-covered pies like Steak, Kidney And Mushroom Pie, as well as Shepherd's Pie with its potato topping. Country recipes like Pork With Plums and Somerset Pork With Apples and old favourites like Liver And Onions offer plenty of variety on the mainstay roasts and casseroles.

OXTAIL BRAISED IN RED WINE

Always plan to cook oxtail 1–2 days before you wish to eat it. This gives you time to skim off the fat before serving.

INGREDIENTS

Serves 3–4
60ml/4 tbsp sunflower oil
1 oxtail (about 1kg/2¼ lb), cut in pieces
2 onions
2 carrots, quartered
2 celery sticks, cut in pieces
300ml/½ pint/1¼ cups beef stock
300ml/½ pint/1¼ cups red wine
bouquet garni
15g/½ oz/1 tbsp plain flour
225g/8oz can chopped tomatoes
salt and black pepper
15ml/1 tbsp chopped fresh parsley, to garnish

1 Heat half the oil in a large flame-proof casserole or ovenproof pan with a tight-fitting lid. Sauté the pieces of oxtail until well browned.

2 Preheat the oven to 160°C/325°F/Gas 3. Add one of the onions, sliced, the pieces of carrot and celery, the stock, wine, bouquet garni, and seasoning. Bring to the boil and then cook in the oven for 1 hour.

3 Baste and stir well, reduce the oven temperature to 150°C/300°F/Gas 2 for 1½–2 hours, or until the meat is very tender. Remove from the oven.

4 Leave to cool completely, then discard the surface fat and reheat. Remove the oxtail and reserve. Strain the stock; discard the vegetables. Preheat the oven to 180°C/350°F/Gas 4.

5 Fry the remaining onion, sliced, with the remaining oil in a large pan until golden. Stir in the flour and cook, stirring, until turning golden.

6 Gradually stir in the stock, a little at a time as it thickens. Bring back to the boil and then stir in the tomatoes. Add the oxtail, and seasoning to taste. Cover and cook in the oven for 30 minutes, or until the oxtail is heated through and really tender. Serve hot, sprinkled with the fresh parsley.

BRAISED BRISKET WITH DUMPLINGS

Brisket is very underrated and most often eaten as salt beef or pastrami these days. Given plenty of gentle cooking it produces a deliciously tender pot roast for eating hot with dumplings, or to serve cold with baked potatoes and salad.

INGREDIENTS

Serves 6–8
15ml/1 tbsp sunflower oil
2 onions, sliced
900g/2 lb piece of rolled brisket, tied
300ml/½ pint/1¼ cups hot beef stock
300ml/½ pint/1¼ cups beer
2 bay leaves
few parsley stalks
2 parsnips, chopped
2 carrots, sliced
½ swede, chopped

For the dumplings
25g/1oz/2 tbsp butter
175g/6oz/1½ cups self-raising flour, sifted
5ml/1 tsp dry mustard powder
5ml/1 tsp each dried sage, thyme and parsley
salt and black pepper
fresh herb sprigs, such as parsley, oregano or thyme, to garnish

1 Preheat the oven to 160°C/325°F/ Gas 3. Heat the oil in a large flameproof casserole or ovenproof pan and fry the onions until well browned.

2 Place the meat on top, then add the hot stock, the beer, bay leaves and parsley stalks and bring to the boil. Cover and transfer to the oven for 2 hours, basting occasionally.

3 Meanwhile, prepare the vegetables and make the dumplings. Rub the butter into the flour, then mix in the mustard powder, herbs and seasoning, and add sufficient water to mix to a soft dough mixture. Shape into about 12 small balls.

4 When the meat is just about tender, add the vegetables and cook for 20 minutes. Check the seasoning, add the dumplings and continue cooking for 15 minutes, until they are nicely swollen. Serve hot, garnished with herb sprigs.

BEEF IN GUINNESS

— INGREDIENTS —

Serves 6

1kg/2lb chuck steak, cut into 4cm/
1½in cubes
plain (all-purpose) flour, for coating
45ml/3 tbsp oil
1 large onion, sliced
1 carrot, thinly sliced
2 celery sticks, thinly sliced
10ml/2 tsp sugar
5ml/1 tsp English mustard powder
15ml/1 tbsp tomato purée (paste)
2.5 x 7.5 cm/1 x 3 in strip orange rind
bouquet garni
600ml/1 pint/2½ cups Guinness
salt and pepper

1 Toss the beef in flour to coat. Heat 30ml/2 tbsp oil in a large, shallow pan, then cook the beef in batches until lightly browned. Transfer to a bowl.

2 Add the remaining oil to the pan, then cook the onions until well browned, adding the carrot and celery towards the end.

3 Stir in the sugar, mustard, tomato purée (paste), orange rind, Guinness and seasoning, then add the bouquet garni and bring to the boil. Return the meat, and any juices in the bowl, to the pan; add water, if necessary, so the meat is covered. Cover the pan tightly and cook gently for 2–2½ hours, until the meat is very tender.

STEAK, KIDNEY AND MUSHROOM PIE

— INGREDIENTS —

Serves 4

30ml/2 tbsp oil
1 onion chopped
115g/4oz bacon, chopped
500g/1¼ lb chuck steak, diced
30ml/2 tbsp plain (all-purpose) flour
115g/4oz lambs' kidneys
400ml/14fl oz/1⅔ cups beef stock
large bouquet garni
115g/4oz button mushrooms
225g/8oz ready-made puff pastry
beaten egg, to glaze
salt and pepper

1 Preheat the oven to 160°C/325°F/ Gas 3. Heat the oil in a heavy-based pan, then cook the bacon and onion until lightly browned.

2 Toss the steak in the flour. Stir the meat into the pan in batches and cook, stirring, until browned.

3 Toss the kidneys in flour and add to to the pan with the bouquet garni. Transfer to a casserole dish, then pour in the stock, cover and cook in the oven for 2 hours. Stir in the mushrooms and seasoning and leave to cool.

4 Preheat the oven to 220°C/425°F/ Gas 7. Roll out the pastry to 2cm/ ¾ in larger than the top of a 1.2 litre/2 pint/5 cup pie dish. Cut off a narrow strip from the pastry and fit around the dampened rim of the dish. Brush the pastry strip with water.

5 Tip the meat mixture, into the dish. Lay the pastry over the dish, press the edges together to seal, then knock them up with the back of a knife.

6 Make a small slit in the pastry, brush with beaten egg and bake for 20 minutes. Lower the oven temperature to 180°C/350°F/Gas 4 and bake for a further 20 minutes, until the pastry is risen, golden and crisp.

BEEF POT ROAST

INGREDIENTS

Serves 8

1.75kg/4lb joint beef suitable for pot
   roasting, such as brisket
3 garlic cloves, cut in half or in thirds
225g/8oz piece salt pork or bacon
275g/10oz/2 cups onions, chopped
3 celery sticks, chopped
2 carrots, chopped
115g/4oz turnip, diced
475ml/16fl oz/2 cups beef or
   chicken stock
475ml/16fl oz/2 cups dry red or
   white wine
1 bay leaf
5ml/1 tsp fresh thyme, or 2.5ml/½ tsp
   dried
4–6 small whole potatoes, or 3 large
   potatoes, quartered
50g/2oz/4 tbsp butter or margarine, at
   room temperature
25g/1oz/¼ cup plain flour
salt and black pepper
watercress, to garnish

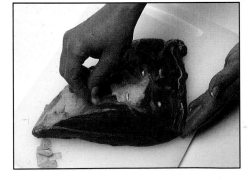

1 Preheat the oven to 160°C/325°F/
Gas 3. Make deep incisions in the
beef joint on all sides with the tip of a
small sharp knife and insert the garlic
pieces.

2 In a large flameproof casserole,
cook the salt pork or bacon over a
low heat until the fat runs and the pork
or bacon begins to brown.

3 Remove the salt pork with a slotted
spoon and discard. Increase the
heat to medium-high and add the beef
joint. Brown it evenly on all sides.
Remove and set aside on a plate or dish.

4 Add the onions, celery and carrots
to the casserole and cook for 8–10
minutes, until softened. Stir in the
turnips, add the stock, wine and herbs
and mix well. Return the joint and any
juices to the casserole, cover and cook
in the oven for 2 hours.

5 Add the potatoes to the casserole,
pushing them down under the
other vegetables. Season with salt and
pepper. Cover and cook for about 45
minutes, until the potatoes are tender.

6 Combine the butter or margarine
with the flour in a small bowl and
mash together to make a paste.

7 Transfer the meat to a warmed
serving dish. Remove the potatoes
and other vegetables from the casserole
with a slotted spoon and arrange
around the joint. Keep warm.

8 Discard the bay leaf, then tilt the
casserole and skim off the excess
fat from the cooking liquid. Bring to the
boil on the hob. Add half of the butter
and flour paste and whisk to blend.
Cook for 3–4 minutes, until the gravy is
thickened. Add more of the paste if
necessary. Strain into a gravy boat.
Serve the meat sliced with the
vegetables and the sauce poured over.
Garnish with watercress.

VARIATION
Add 175g/6oz frozen peas to the
casserole about 5 minutes before
the potatoes are cooked.

Shepherd's Pie

Ingredients

Serves 4

30ml/2 tbsp oil
1 onion, finely chopped
1 carrot, finely chopped
115g/4oz mushrooms, chopped
500g/1¼lb lean chuck steak, minced (ground)
300ml/½ pint/1¼ cups brown veal stock or water
15ml/1 tbsp plain (all-purpose) flour
bay leaf
10–15ml/2–3 tsp Worcestershire sauce
15ml/1 tbsp tomato purée (paste)
675g/1½lb potatoes, boiled
25g/1oz/2 tbsp butter
45ml/3 tbsp hot milk
15ml/1 tbsp chopped fresh tarragon
salt and pepper

1 Heat the oil in a saucepan, add the onion, carrot and mushrooms and cook, stirring occasionally, until browned. Stir the beef into the pan and cook, stirring to break up the lumps, until lightly browned.

2 Blend a few spoonfuls of the stock or water with the flour, then stir this mixture into the pan. Stir in the remaining stock or water and bring to a simmer, stirring. Add the bay leaf, Worcestershire sauce and tomato purée (paste), then cover and cook very gently for 1 hour, stirring occasionally. Uncover the pan towards the end of cooking to allow any excess water to evaporate, if necessary.

3 Preheat the oven to 190°C/375°F/ Gas 5. Gently heat the potatoes for a couple of minutes, then mash with the butter, milk and seasoning.

4 Add the tarragon and seasoning to the mince, then pour into a pie dish. Cover the mince with an even layer of potato and mark the top with the prongs of a fork. Bake for about 25 minutes, until golden brown.

IRISH STEW

Serves 4
4 slices smoked streaky bacon,
   chopped
2 celery sticks, chopped
2 large onions, sliced
8 middle neck lamb chops, about
   1kg/2lb total weight
1kg/2lb potatoes, sliced
300ml/½ pint/1¼ cups brown veal
   stock or water
22.5ml/1½ tbsp Worcestershire sauce
5ml/1 tsp anchovy sauce
salt and pepper
chopped fresh parsley, to garnish

1 Preheat the oven to 160°C/325°F/ Gas 3. Fry the bacon for 3–5 minutes until the fat runs, then add the celery and a third of the onions and cook, stirring occasionally, until browned.

2 Layer the lamb chops, potatoes, vegetables and bacon and remaining onions in a heavy flameproof casserole, seasoning each layer, and finishing with a layer of potatoes.

3 Stir the veal stock or water, Worcestershire sauce and anchovy sauce into the bacon and vegetable cooking juices in the pan and bring to the boil. Pour into the casserole, adding water if necessary so the liquid comes half way up the casserole.

4 Cover the casserole tightly, then cook in the oven for 3 hours, until the meat and vegetables are tender. Serve hot, sprinkled with chopped fresh parsley.

COOK'S TIP
The mutton that originally gave the flavour to Irish Stew is often difficult to obtain nowadays, so other flavourings are added to compensate.

SQUAB PIE

INGREDIENTS

Serves 4

675g/1½lb lamb neck fillets, cut into 12
  pieces
115g/4oz gammon, diced
1 onion, thinly sliced
350g/12oz leeks, sliced
1 large cooking apple, peeled, cored
  and sliced
1.25–2.5ml/¼–½tsp ground allspice
1.25–2.5ml/¼–½tsp freshly grated
  nutmeg
150ml/¼ pint/⅔ cup lamb, beef or
  vegetable stock
225g/8oz ready-made shortcrust (pie)
  pastry
beaten egg or milk, to glaze
salt and pepper

1 Preheat the oven to 200°C/400°F/ Gas 6. Layer the meats, onion, leeks and apple in a 900ml/1½ pint/3¾ cup pie dish, sprinkling in the spices and seasoning as you go. Pour in the stock.

2 Roll out the pastry to 2cm/¾ in larger than the top of the pie dish. Cut a narrow strip from around the pastry, fit it around the dampened rim of the dish, then brush with water.

3 Lay the pastry over the dish, and press the edges together to seal them. Brush the top with beaten egg or milk, and make a hole in the centre.

4 Bake the pie for 20 minutes, then reduce the oven temperature to 180°C/350°F/Gas 4 and continue to bake for 1-1¼ hours, covering the pie with foil if the pastry begins to become too brown.

BEEF WELLINGTON

Beef Wellington is supposedly so-named because of the resemblance of its shape and rich brown colour to the Duke of Wellington's boot.

INGREDIENTS

Serves 8

1.4kg/3lb fillet of beef
15g/½oz/1 tbsp butter
30ml/2 tbsp oil
½ small onion, finely chopped
175g/6oz mushrooms, chopped
175g/6oz liver pâté
lemon juice
few drops of Worcestershire sauce
400g/14oz ready-made puff pastry
salt and pepper
beaten egg, to glaze

1 Preheat the oven to 220°C/425°F/ Gas 7. Season the beef with pepper, then tie it at intervals with string.

2 Heat the butter and oil in a roasting tin (pan). Brown the beef over a high heat, then cook in the oven for 20 minutes. Cool and remove the string.

3 Scrape the cooking juices into a pan, add the onion and mushrooms and cook until tender. Cool, then mix with the pâté. Add lemon juice and Worcestershire sauce.

4 Roll out the pastry to a large 5mm/¼ in thick rectangle. Spread the pâté mixture on the beef, then place it in the centre of the pastry. Damp the edges of the pastry, then fold over to make a neat parcel, tucking in the ends neatly; press to seal.

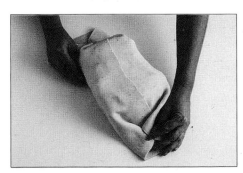

5 Place the parcel on a baking (cookie) sheet with the join underneath and brush with beaten egg. Bake for 25–45 minutes, depending how well done you like the beef to be.

FARMHOUSE VENISON PIE

A simple and satisfying pie –
venison in a rich gravy, topped
with potato and parsnip mash.

INGREDIENTS

Serves 4

45ml/3 tbsp sunflower oil
1 onion, chopped
1 garlic clove, crushed
3 rashers streaky bacon, rinded and
   chopped
675g/1½lb minced venison
115g/4oz button mushrooms, chopped
30ml/2 tbsp plain flour
450ml/¾ pint/1⅞ cups beef stock
150ml/¼ pint/⅔ cup ruby port
2 bay leaves
5ml/1 tsp chopped fresh thyme
5ml/1 tsp Dijon mustard
15ml/1 tbsp redcurrant jelly
675g/1½lb potatoes
450g/1lb parsnips
1 egg yolk
50g/2oz/4 tbsp butter
freshly grated nutmeg
45ml/3 tbsp chopped fresh parsley
salt and black pepper

1 Heat the oil in a large frying pan
and fry the onion, garlic and bacon
for about 5 minutes. Add the venison
and mushrooms and cook for a few
minutes, stirring, until browned.

2 Stir in the flour and cook for 1–2
minutes, then add the stock, port,
herbs, mustard, redcurrant jelly and
seasoning. Bring to the boil, cover
and simmer for 30–40 minutes, until
tender. Spoon into a large pie dish or
four individual ovenproof dishes.

3 While the venison and mushroom
mixture is cooking, preheat the oven
to 200°C/400°F/Gas 6. Cut the potatoes and parsnips into large chunks.
Cook together in boiling salted water for
20 minutes or until tender. Drain and
mash, then beat in the egg yolk, butter,
nutmeg, chopped parsley and seasoning.

4 Spread the potato and parsnip
mixture over the meat and bake for
30–40 minutes, until piping hot and
golden brown. Serve at once.

MINCED BEEF PIE WITH GARLIC POTATOES

This is almost a complete meal in itself, but you could add lots more vegetables to the meat to make it go further.

---INGREDIENTS---

Serves 4

450g/1 lb lean minced beef
1 onion, chopped
3 carrots, sliced
4 tomatoes, peeled and chopped
300ml/½ pint/1¼ cups beef stock
5ml/1 tsp cornflour
15ml/1 tbsp chopped, mixed herbs, or
    5ml/1 tsp dried
30ml/2 tbsp olive oil
2 garlic cloves, crushed
500g/1¼ lb potatoes (3 large), par-
    cooked and sliced
salt and black pepper

1 Preheat the oven to 180°C/350°F/ Gas 4. Stir-fry the meat and onions in a large pan until browned. Add the carrots and tomatoes to the pan.

2 Stir in the stock, with the cornflour blended in, and the herbs. Bring to the boil and simmer for 2–3 minutes, then season to taste. Transfer to a shallow ovenproof dish.

3 Mix the oil, garlic and seasoning together. Layer the potatoes on top of the meat mixture, brushing liberally with the garlic oil. Cook for 30–40 minutes, until the potatoes are tender and golden. Serve with a green salad and crisp green beans or mange-tout.

COOK'S TIP
Leave the potatoes unpeeled, if you prefer, in this recipe, and incorporate other par-cooked root vegetables such as carrot, celeriac, swede or turnip, and layer them with the potatoes.

LANCASHIRE HOTPOT

Browning the lamb and kidneys, plus all the extra vegetables and herbs, add flavour to the traditional basic ingredients.

INGREDIENTS

Serves 4
40g/1½oz/3 tbsp dripping, or 45ml/
3 tbsp oil
8 middle neck lamb chops, about
1kg/2lb total weight
175g/6oz lambs' kidneys, cut into
large pieces
1kg/2lb potatoes, thinly sliced
3 carrots, thickly sliced
450g/1lb leeks, sliced
3 celery sticks, sliced
15ml/1 tbsp chopped fresh thyme
30ml/2 tbsp chopped fresh parsley
small sprig of rosemary
600ml/1 pint/2½ cups veal stock
salt and pepper

1 Preheat the oven to 170°C/325°F/ Gas 3. Heat the dripping or oil in a frying pan and brown the chops and kidneys in batches, then reserve the fat.

2 In a large casserole, make alternate layers of lamb chops, kidneys, three-quarters of the potatoes and the carrots, leeks and celery, sprinkling the herbs and seasoning over each layer as you go. Tuck the rosemary sprig down the side.

3 Arrange the remaining potatoes on top. Pour over the stock, brush with the reserved fat, then cover and bake for 2½ hours. Increase the oven temperature to 220°C/425°F/Gas 7. Uncover and cook for 30 minutes.

PORK WITH PLUMS

INGREDIENTS

Serves 4
450g/1lb ripe plums, halved and
stoned (pitted)
300ml/½ pint/1¼ cups apple juice
40g/1½oz/3 tbsp butter
15ml/1 tbsp oil
4 pork chops, about 200g/7oz each
1 onion, finely chopped
freshly ground mace
salt and pepper
fresh sage leave, to garnish

1 Heat the butter and oil in a large frying pan and fry the chops until brown on both sides, then transfer them to a plate.

2 Meanwhile, simmer the plums in the apple juice until tender. Strain off and reserve the juice, then purée half the plums with a little of the juice.

3 Add the onion to the pan and cook gently until soft, but not coloured. Return the chops to the pan. Pour over the plum purée and all the juice.

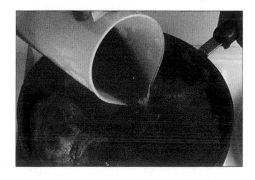

4 Simmer, uncovered, for 10–15 minutes, until the chops are cooked through. Add the remaining plums to the pan, then add the mace and seasoning. Warm the sauce through over a medium heat and serve garnished with fresh sage leaves.

COOK'S TIP
Use boneless pork steaks in place of the chops, if you like.

Country Meat Loaf

Serves 6

25g/1oz/2 tbsp butter or margarine
½ onion, finely chopped
2 garlic cloves, finely chopped
2 celery sticks, finely chopped
450g/1lb lean minced beef
225g/8oz minced veal
225g/8oz lean minced pork
2 eggs
50g/2oz/1 cup fresh white
*   breadcrumbs*
90ml/6 tbsp chopped fresh parsley
30ml/2 tbsp chopped fresh basil
2.5ml/½ tsp fresh or dried thyme
30ml/2 tbsp Worcestershire sauce
45ml/3 tbsp chilli sauce
6 streaky bacon rashers
salt and black pepper
fresh basil and parsley sprigs,
*   to garnish*

1 Preheat the oven to 180°C/350°F/ Gas 4. Melt the butter or margarine in a small frying pan over a low heat. Add the onion, garlic and celery and cook for 8–10 minutes, until softened. Remove the frying pan from the heat and leave to cool slightly.

2 Tip the onion mixture into a large bowl and add all the other ingredients except the bacon. Mix together lightly, using a fork or your fingers. Do not overwork or the meat loaf will be too compact.

3 Form the meat mixture into an oval loaf. Carefully transfer it to a shallow baking tin.

4 Lay the bacon rashers across the meat loaf. Bake for 1¼ hours, basting occasionally with the juices and bacon fat in the tin. Remove the meat loaf from the oven and drain off the fat. Leave to stand for 10 minutes. Garnish with basil and parsley and serve.

LIVER AND ONIONS

Calves' liver is wonderfully tender and makes this simple dish mouthwateringly delicious. However it is expensive so substitute thinly sliced lambs' liver, if you prefer and cook over a low heat until just tender.

INGREDIENTS

Serves 4
60ml/4 tbsp oil
3 large onions, total weight about
 600g/1lb 6oz, sliced
450g/1lb calves' liver, cut into 5mm/
 ¼in thick slices
salt and pepper
sage leaves, to garnish

1 Heat 45 ml/3 tbsp of the oil in a large, heavy frying pan. Add the onions and a little seasoning, cover and cook over a low heat, stirring occasionally, for 25–30 minutes, until the onions are soft.

2 Uncover the pan, increase the heat to medium-high and cook the onions, stirring, for 5–7 minutes until golden. Using a slotted spoon, transfer to a bowl, leaving the oil in the pan.

3 Add the remaining oil to the pan and increase the heat to high. Working in batches so the liver is in a single layer, cook for 45–60 seconds a side until just browned on the outside, and pink inside and tender. Season, then transfer to a warm plate and keep warm while frying the remaining liver in the same way.

4 Return all the liver and the onions to the pan and cook over a high heat for 30–60 seconds. Serve at once, garnished with sage.

COOK'S TIP
The onions need to be covered during their initial cooking, if your frying pan does not have a lid, use foil as a cover.

VENISON WITH CRANBERRY SAUCE

Venison steaks are now readily available. Lean and low in fat, they make a healthy choice for a special occasion. Served with a sauce of fresh seasonal cranberries, port and ginger, they make a dish with a wonderful combination of flavours.

INGREDIENTS

Serves 4
1 orange
1 lemon
75g/3oz/1 cup fresh or frozen
  cranberries
5ml/1 tsp grated fresh root ginger
1 thyme sprig
5ml/1 tsp Dijon mustard
60ml/4 tbsp redcurrant jelly
150ml/¼ pint/⅔ cup ruby port
30ml/2 tbsp sunflower oil
4 venison steaks
2 shallots, finely chopped
salt and black pepper
thyme sprigs, to garnish
creamy mashed potatoes and broccoli,
  to serve

1 Pare the rind from half the orange and half the lemon using a vegetable peeler, then cut into very fine strips.

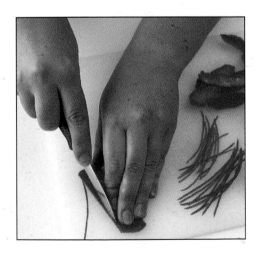

2 Blanch the strips in a small pan of boiling water for about 5 minutes until tender. Drain the strips and refresh under cold water.

3 Squeeze the juice from the orange and lemon and then pour into a small pan. Add the fresh or frozen cranberries, ginger, thyme sprig, mustard, redcurrant jelly and port. Cook over a low heat until the jelly melts.

4 Bring the sauce to the boil, stirring occasionally, then cover the pan and reduce the heat. Cook gently, for about 15 minutes, until the cranberries are just tender.

5 Heat the oil in a heavy-based frying pan, add the venison steaks and cook over a high heat for 2–3 minutes.

6 Turn over the steaks and add the shallots to the pan. Cook the steaks on the other side for 2–3 minutes, depending on whether you like rare or medium cooked meat.

7 Just before the end of cooking, pour in the sauce and add the strips of orange and lemon rind.

8 Leave the sauce to bubble for a few seconds to thicken slightly, then remove the thyme sprig and adjust the seasoning to taste.

9 Transfer the venison steaks to warmed plates and spoon over the sauce. Garnish with thyme sprigs and serve accompanied by creamy mashed potatoes and broccoli.

COOK'S TIP
When frying venison, always remember the briefer the better; venison will turn to leather if subjected to fierce heat after it has reached the medium-rare stage. If you dislike any hint of pink, cook it to this stage then let it rest in a low oven for a few minutes.

VARIATION
When fresh cranberries are unavailable, use redcurrants instead. Stir them into the sauce towards the end of cooking with the orange and lemon rinds.

PORK BRAISED IN BEER

INGREDIENTS

Serves 6

1.75–2.25kg/4–5¼lb loin of pork, boned, trimmed of excess fat and tied
15ml/1 tbsp butter
15ml/1 tbsp vegetable oil
3 large onions, halved and thinly sliced
1 garlic clove, finely chopped
600ml/1 pint/2½ cups beer
1 bay leaf
15ml/1 tbsp plain flour blended with 30ml/2 tbsp water
salt and black pepper
courgettes, to serve

3 Stir in the beer, scraping to remove any bits on the bottom of the casserole. Add the bay leaf.

4 Return the pork to the casserole. Cover and cook over a low heat for about 2 hours, turning the pork halfway through the cooking time.

5 Remove the pork from the casserole. Slice thickly. Arrange on a platter. Cover and keep warm.

6 Discard the bay leaf. Add the flour mixture to the cooking juices and cook over a high heat, stirring constantly, until thickened. Taste for seasoning. Pour over the pork and serve at once with courgettes.

1 Season the pork on all sides with salt and pepper. Heat the butter and oil in a flameproof casserole just large enough to hold the pork. When hot, add the pork and brown on all sides for 5–7 minutes, turning it to colour evenly. Remove from the casserole and set aside.

2 Drain all but 15ml/1 tbsp fat from the casserole. Add the onions and garlic and cook for about 5 minutes, until just softened.

PORK LOIN WITH CELERY

INGREDIENTS

Serves 4

15ml/1 tbsp oil
50g/2oz/4 tbsp butter
about 1kg/2 lb boned and rolled loin
of pork, rind removed and well
trimmed
1 onion, chopped
bouquet garni
3 sprigs fresh dill (dillweed)
150ml/¼ pint/⅔ cup medium-bodied
dry white wine
150ml/¼ pint/⅔ cup water
sticks from 1 celery head, cut into
2.5cm/1in lengths
30ml/2 tbsp plain (all-purpose) flour
150ml/¼ pint/⅔ cup double (heavy)
cream
squeeze of lemon juice
salt and pepper
chopped fresh dill (dillweed), to
garnish

1 Heat the oil and half the butter in a heavy flameproof casserole just large enough to hold the pork and celery, then add the pork and brown evenly. Transfer the pork to a plate.

2 Add the onion to the casserole and cook until softened but not coloured. Place the bouquet garni and the dill (dillweed) sprigs on the onions, then place the pork on top and add any juices on the plate.

3 Pour the wine and water over the pork, season, cover tightly and simmer gently for 30 minutes.

4 Turn the pork, arrange the celery around it, then re-cover and continue to cook for about 40 minutes, until the pork and celery are tender.

5 Transfer the pork and celery to a warmed serving plate, cover and keep warm. Discard the bouquet garni and dill (dillweed).

6 Mash the remaining butter with the flour, then whisk small pieces at a time into the cooking liquid while it is barely simmering. Cook for 2–3 minutes, stirring occasionally. Stir the cream into the casserole, bring to the boil and add a squeeze of lemon juice.

7 Slice the pork, pour some of the sauce over the slices and garnish with chopped dill (dillweed). Serve the remaining sauce separately.

LAMB WITH MINT SAUCE

INGREDIENTS

Serves 4

8 lamb noisettes, 2–2.5cm/ ¾–1in thick
30ml/2 tbsp oil
45ml/3 tbsp medium-bodied dry white
   wine, or vegetable or veal stock
salt and pepper
sprigs of mint, to garnish

For The Sauce

30ml/2 tbsp boiling water
5–10ml/1–2 tsp sugar
leaves from a small bunch of mint,
   finely chopped
about 30ml/2 tbsp white wine vinegar
salt and pepper

1 For the sauce, stir the water and sugar together, then add the mint, vinegar to taste and seasoning. Leave for 30 minutes.

2 Season the lamb with pepper. Heat the oil in a large frying pan, then fry the lamb, in batches if necessary so the pan is not crowded, for about 3 minutes a side for meat that is pink.

3 Transfer the lamb to a warmed plate and season with salt, then cover and keep warm.

4 Stir the wine or stock into the cooking juices, dislodging the sediment, and bring to the boil. Bubble for a couple of minutes, then pour over the lamb. Garnish the lamb noisettes with small sprigs of mint and serve hot with the Mint Sauce.

SOMERSET PORK WITH APPLES

INGREDIENTS

Serves 4

25g/1oz/2 tbsp butter
500g/1¼lb pork loin, cut into bite-sized
   pieces
12 baby onions, peeled
10ml/2 tsp grated lemon rind
300ml/ ½ pint/1¼ cups dry (hard) cider
150ml/ ¼ pint/ ⅔ cup veal stock
2 crisp eating apples such as Granny
   Smith, cored and sliced
45ml/3 tbsp chopped fresh parsley
100ml/3½ fl oz/scant ½ cup whipping
   cream
salt and pepper

1 Heat the butter in a large sauté or frying pan, then brown the pork in batches. Transfer the pork to a bowl.

2 Add the onions to the pan, brown lightly, then stir in the lemon rind, cider and stock and boil for about 3 minutes. Return all the pork to the pan and cook gently for about 25 minutes, until the pork is tender.

3 Add the apples to the pan and cook for a further 5 minutes. Using a slotted spoon, transfer the pork, onions and apples to a warmed serving dish, cover and keep warm. Stir the parsley and cream into the pan and allow to bubble to thicken the sauce slightly. Season, then pour over the pork and serve hot.

ROAST LAMB WITH MUSHROOM STUFFING

When the thigh bone is removed from a leg of lamb a stuffing can be put in its place. This not only makes the joint easier to carve but also gives an excellent flavour to the meat.

──────── INGREDIENTS ────────

Serves 4
1.75kg/4–4½lb leg of lamb, boned
salt and freshly ground black pepper
watercress, to garnish
roast potatoes, carrots and broccoli,
* to serve*

For The Wild Mushroom Stuffing
25g/1oz/2 tbsp butter
1 shallot or small onion
225g/8oz assorted wild and cultivated
* mushrooms such as chanterelles,*
* ceps, oyster, field mushrooms,*
* trimmed and chopped*
½ garlic clove, crushed
1 sprig thyme, chopped
25g/1oz crustless white bread, diced
2 egg yolks

For The Wild Mushroom Gravy
50ml/2fl oz/¼ cup red wine
400ml/14fl oz/1⅔ cups chicken stock,
* boiling*
5g/⅛oz/2 tbsp dried porcini
* mushrooms, soaked in boiling water*
* for 20 minutes*
20ml/4 tsp cornflour
5ml/1 tsp Dijon mustard
2.5ml/½ tsp wine vinegar
knob of butter

1 Preheat the oven to 200°C/400°F/ Gas 6. To make the mushroom stuffing, melt the butter in a large non-stick frying pan and gently fry the shallot or onion without colouring. Add the mushrooms, garlic and thyme and stir until the mushroom juices begin to run, then increase the heat so that they evaporate completely.

2 Transfer the mushrooms to a mixing bowl, add the bread, egg yolks and seasoning and mix well. Allow to cool slightly.

3 Season the inside cavity of the lamb and then press the stuffing into the cavity, using a spoon or your fingers. Tie up the end with fine string and then tie around the joint so that it does not lose its shape.

4 Place the lamb in a roasting tin and roast in the oven for 15 minutes per 450g/1lb for rare meat and 20 minutes per 450g/1lb for medium-rare. A 1.8kg/ 4lb leg will take 1 hour 20 minutes if cooked medium-rare.

5 Transfer the lamb to a warmed serving plate, cover and keep warm. To make the gravy, spoon off all excess fat from the roasting tin and brown the sediment over a moderate heat. Add the wine and stir with a flat wooden spoon to loosen the sediment. Add the chicken stock, the mushrooms and their soaking liquid.

6 Place the cornflour and mustard in a cup and blend with 15 ml/1 tsp water. Stir into the stock and simmer to thicken. Add the vinegar. Season to taste, and stir in the butter. Garnish the lamb with watercress, and serve with roast potatoes, carrots and broccoli.

LAMB AND SPRING VEGETABLE STEW

You could also add a few blanched asparagus spears or young green beans to this version of the creamy-coloured stew known as a *blanquette*.

INGREDIENTS

Serves 4

65g/2½oz/5 tbsp butter
1kg/2lb lean boneless shoulder of lamb, cut into 4cm/1½in cubes
600ml/1 pint/2½ cups lamb stock or water
150ml/¼ pint/⅔ cup dry white wine
1 onion, quartered
2 thyme sprigs
1 bay leaf
225g/8oz baby onions, halved
225g/8oz small young carrots
2 small turnips, quartered
175g/6oz shelled broad beans
15ml/1 tbsp plain flour
1 egg yolk
45ml/3 tbsp double cream
10ml/2 tsp lemon juice
salt and black pepper
30ml/2 tbsp chopped fresh parsley, to garnish

1 Melt 25g/1oz/2 tbsp of the butter in a large pan, add the lamb and sauté for about 2 minutes to seal the meat; do not allow it to colour.

2 Pour in the stock or water and wine, bring to the boil, then skim the surface. Add the quartered onion, thyme and bay leaf. Cover and simmer for 1 hour.

3 Meanwhile, melt 15g/½oz/1 tbsp of the remaining butter in a frying pan over a moderate heat, add the baby onions and brown lightly.

4 Add the browned baby onions, carrots and turnips to the lamb and continue to cook for 20 minutes. Add the shelled broad beans and cook for a further 10 minutes, until the vegetables and lamb are tender.

5 Lift out the lamb and vegetables from the pan and arrange in a warmed serving dish. Cover and keep warm in low oven.

6 Discard the onion quarters and herbs. Strain the stock and carefully skim off all the fat. Return the stock to the pan and boil rapidly over a high heat until the liquid has reduced to 450ml/¾ pint/1⅞ cups.

7 Mix the remaining butter and the flour together to form a smooth paste. Whisk into the hot stock until thickened. Simmer for 2–3 minutes.

8 Blend together the egg yolk and cream in a bowl. Stir in a little of the hot sauce, then stir this back into the sauce. Reheat gently but do not boil. Add the lemon juice and season to taste with salt and pepper.

9 Pour the sauce over the lamb and vegetables, then sprinkle with the chopped parsley. Serve at once.

COOK'S TIP
The appearance of this dish improves if the tough outer skin of the shelled broad beans is removed to reveal the bright green colour. Blanch the beans for 1 minute in boiling water, drain and refresh, then slit the skins and squeeze out the inner beans.

POULTRY AND GAME

At one time almost every household kept at least a few chickens, so it is not surprising that British cooks created an enormous repertoire of chicken dishes. The birds were a source of cheap protein food and provided eggs for the family or for sale. With industrialization, domestic poultry-keeping almost disappeared, and chicken became something of a luxury, but commercial poultry farms now put within everyone's reach not only the classic Stuffed Roast Chicken, but a range of pies such as Chicken Charter Pie and Chicken And Ham Pie, casserole dishes such as Chicken In Green Sauce and Stoved Chicken, as well as Spatchcocked Devilled Poussins and many more. Commercial farming has also made available much game meat and the ingredients for classics like Pot-Roast of Venison are now to be found on the supermarket shelves.

ROAST CHICKEN WITH CELERIAC

INGREDIENTS

Serves 4
1.6kg/3½ lb chicken
15g/½oz/1 tbsp butter

For The Stuffing
450g/1 lb celeriac (celery root),
   chopped
25g/1oz/2 tbsp butter
3 slices bacon, chopped
1 onion, finely chopped
leaves from 1 thyme sprig, chopped
leaves from 1 small tarragon sprig,
   chopped
30ml/2 tbsp chopped fresh parsley
75g/3oz/1½ cups fresh brown breadcrumbs
dash of Worcestershire sauce
1 egg
salt and pepper

1 To make the stuffing, cook the celeriac (celery root) in boiling water
until tender. Drain well and chop finely.

2 Heat the butter in a saucepan, then
gently cook the bacon and onion
until the onion is soft. Stir the celeriac
(celery root) and herbs into the pan
and cook, stirring occasionally, for 2–3
minutes. Meanwhile, preheat the oven
to 200°C/400°F/Gas 6.

3 Remove the pan from the heat and
stir in the fresh breadcrumbs,
Worcestershire sauce, seasoning and
sufficient egg to bind. Use to stuff the
neck end of the chicken. Season the
bird's skin, then rub with the butter.

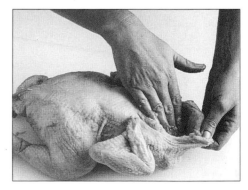

COOK'S TIP
Roll any excess stuffing into small
balls and bake in an ovenproof
dish with the chicken for 20–30
minutes until golden brown.

4 Roast the chicken, basting occasionally with the juices, for 1¼–1½
hours, until the juices run clear when
the thickest part of the leg is pierced.

5 Turn off the oven, prop the door
open slightly and allow the chicken
to rest for 10 minutes before carving.

STOVED CHICKEN

'Stoved' is derived from the French *étouffer* – to cook in a covered pot – and originates from the Franco/Scottish 'Alliance' of the seventeenth century.

INGREDIENTS

Serves 4

1kg/2 lb potatoes, cut into 5mm/¼ in slices
2 large onions, thinly sliced
15ml/1 tbsp chopped fresh thyme
25g/1oz/2 tbsp butter
15ml/1 tbsp oil
2 large slices bacon, chopped
4 large chicken joints, halved
bay leaf
600ml/1 pint/2½ cups chicken stock
salt and pepper

1 Preheat the oven to 150°C/300°F/ Gas 2. Make a thick layer of half the potato slices in the bottom of a large, heavy casserole, then cover with half the onion. Sprinkle with half the thyme, and seasonings.

COOK'S TIP
Instead of buying large chicken joints and cutting them in half, choose either chicken thighs or chicken drumsticks – or use a mixture of the two.

2 Heat the butter and oil in a large frying pan, then brown the bacon and chicken. Using a slotted spoon, transfer the chicken and bacon to the casserole. Reserve the fat in the pan.

3 Sprinkle the remaining thyme and some seasoning over the chicken, then cover with the remaining onion, followed by a neat layer of overlapping potato slices. Sprinkle with seasoning.

4 Pour the stock into the casserole, brush the potatoes with the reserved fat, then cover tightly and cook in the oven for about 2 hours, until the chicken is tender.

5 Preheat the grill (broiler). Uncover the casserole and place under the grill (broiler) and cook until the slices of potato are beginning to brown and crisp. Serve hot.

CHICKEN, CARROT AND LEEK PARCELS

These intriguing parcels may sound a bit fiddly for everyday, but they take very little time and you can freeze them – ready to cook gently from frozen.

INGREDIENTS

Serves 4
4 chicken fillets or boneless breast
* portions*
2 small leeks, sliced
2 carrots, grated
4 stoned black olives, chopped
1 garlic clove, crushed
15–30ml/1–2 tbsp olive oil
8 anchovy fillets
salt and black pepper
black olives and herb sprigs, to garnish

1 Preheat the oven to 200°C/400°F/ Gas 6. Season the chicken well.

2 Divide the leeks equally among four sheets of greased greaseproof paper, about 23cm/9 in square. Place a piece of chicken on top of each.

3 Mix the carrots, olives, garlic and oil together. Season lightly and place on top of the chicken portions. Top each with two of the anchovy fillets, then carefully wrap up each parcel, making sure the paper folds are underneath and the carrot mixture on top.

4 Bake for 20 minutes and serve hot, in the paper, garnished with black olives and herb sprigs.

CHICKEN IN A TOMATO COAT

INGREDIENTS

Serves 4–6
1.5–1.75kg/3½– 4 lb free-range chicken
1 small onion
knob of butter
75ml/5 tbsp ready-made tomato sauce
30ml/2 tbsp chopped, mixed fresh
* herbs, such as parsley, tarragon, sage,*
* basil and marjoram, or 10ml/2 tsp*
* dried*
small glass of dry white wine
2–3 small tomatoes, sliced
olive oil
little cornflour (optional)
salt and black pepper

1 Preheat the oven to 190°C/375°F/ Gas 5. Wash and wipe dry the chicken and place in a roasting tin. Place the onion, a knob of butter and some seasoning inside the chicken.

2 Spread most of the tomato sauce over the chicken and sprinkle with half the herbs and some seasoning. Pour the wine into the roasting tin.

3 Cover with foil, then roast for 1½ hours, basting occasionally. Remove the foil, spread with the remaining sauce and the sliced tomatoes and drizzle with oil. Continue cooking for a further 20–30 minutes, or until the chicken is cooked through.

4 Sprinkle the remaining herbs over the chicken, then carve into portions. Thicken the sauce with a little cornflour if you wish. Serve hot.

CHICKEN WITH LEMON AND HERBS

The herbs can be changed according to what is available; for example, parsley or thyme could be used instead of tarragon and fennel.

INGREDIENTS

Serves 2

50g/2oz/4 tbsp butter
*2 spring onions (scallions), white part
  only, finely chopped*
15ml/1 tbsp chopped fresh tarragon
15ml/1 tbsp chopped fresh fennel
juice of 1 lemon
4 chicken thighs
salt and pepper
lemon slices and herb sprigs, to garnish

1 Preheat the grill (broiler) to moderate. In a small saucepan, melt the butter, then add the spring onions (scallions), herbs, lemon juice and seasoning.

2 Brush the chicken thighs generously with the herb mixture, then grill (broil) for 10–12 minutes, basting frequently with the herb mixture.

3 Turn over the chicken and baste again, then cook for a further 10–12 minutes or until the chicken juices run clear.

4 Serve the chicken garnished with lemon slices and herb sprigs, and accompanied by any remaining herb mixture.

CHICKEN WITH RED CABBAGE

INGREDIENTS

Serves 4

50g/2oz/4 tbsp butter
4 large chicken portions, halved
1 onion, chopped
*500g/1¼ lb red cabbage, finely
  shredded*
4 juniper berries, crushed
12 cooked chestnuts
*120ml/4 fl oz/½ cup full-bodied red
  wine*
salt and pepper

1 Heat the butter in a heavy flameproof casserole and lightly brown the chicken pieces. Transfer to a plate.

2 Add the onion to the casserole and fry gently until soft and light golden brown. Stir the cabbage and juniper berries into the casserole, season and cook over a moderate heat for 6–7 minutes, stirring once or twice.

3 Stir the chestnuts into the casserole, then tuck the chicken pieces under the cabbage so they are on the bottom of the casserole. Pour in the red wine.

4 Cover and cook gently for about 40 minutes until the chicken juices run clear and the cabbage is very tender. Check the seasoning and serve.

CHICKEN IN GREEN SAUCE

Slow, gentle cooking makes the chicken succulent and tender.

INGREDIENTS

Serves 4
25g/1oz/2 tbsp butter
15ml/1 tbsp olive oil
4 chicken portions
1 small onion, finely chopped
150ml/¼ pint/⅔ cup medium-bodied
  dry white wine
150ml/¼ pint/⅔ cup chicken stock
175g/6oz watercress, leaves removed
leaves from 2 thyme sprigs and 2
  tarragon sprigs
150ml/¼ pint/⅔ cup double (heavy)
  cream
salt and pepper
watercress leaves, to garnish

1 Heat the butter and oil in a heavy shallow pan, then brown the chicken evenly. Transfer the chicken to a plate using a slotted spoon and keep warm in the oven.

2 Add the onion to the cooking juices in the pan and cook until softened but not coloured.

3 Stir in the wine, boil for 2–3 minutes, then add the stock and bring to the boil. Return the chicken to the pan, cover tightly and cook very gently for about 30 minutes, until the chicken juices run clear. Then transfer the chicken to a warm dish, cover the dish and keep warm.

4 Boil the cooking juices hard until reduced to about 60ml/4 tbsp. Remove the leaves from the watercress and herbs, add to the pan with the cream and simmer over a medium heat until slightly thickened.

5 Return the chicken to the casserole, season and heat through for a few minutes. Garnish with watercress leaves to serve.

COOK'S TIP
Use boneless turkey steaks in place of the chicken portions in this recipe, if you prefer.

SPATCHCOCKED DEVILLED POUSSINS

'Spatchcock', perhaps a corruption of the old Irish phrase 'despatch a cock', refers to birds that are split and skewered flat for cooking.

---INGREDIENTS---

Serves 4
15ml/1 tbsp English mustard powder
15ml/1 tbsp paprika
15ml/1 tbsp ground cumin
20ml/4 tsp tomato ketchup (catsup)
15ml/1 tbsp lemon juice
65g/2½oz/5 tbsp butter, melted
4 poussins, about 450g/1 lb each
salt

1 Mix together the mustard, paprika, cumin, ketchup (catsup), lemon juice and salt until smooth, then gradually stir in the butter.

2 Using game shears or strong kitchen scissors, split each poussin along one side of the backbone, then cut down the other side of the backbone to remove it.

3 Open out a poussin, skin side uppermost, then press down firmly with the heel of your hand. Pass a long skewer through one leg and out through the other to secure the bird open and flat. Repeat with the remaining birds.

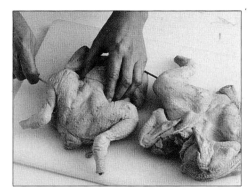

4 Spread the mustard mixture evenly over the skin of the birds. Cover loosely and leave in a cool place for at least 2 hours. Preheat a grill (broiler).

5 Place the birds, skin side uppermost, under the grill (broiler) and cook for about 12 minutes. Turn the birds over, baste with any juices in the pan, and cook for a further 7 minutes, until the juices run clear.

COOK'S TIP
Spatchcocked poussins cook very well on the barbecue, make sure the coals are very hot, then cook for 15–20 minutes, turning and basting frequently.

RABBIT WITH MUSTARD

INGREDIENTS

Serves 4
15ml/1 tbsp plain (all-purpose) flour
15ml/1 tbsp English mustard powder
4 large rabbit joints
25g/1oz/2 tbsp butter
30ml/2 tbsp oil
1 onion, finely chopped
150ml/¼ pint/⅔ cup beer
300ml/½ pint/1¼ cups chicken or veal
    stock
15ml/1 tbsp tarragon vinegar
30ml/2 tbsp dark brown sugar
10–15ml/2–3 tsp prepared English
    mustard
salt and pepper

To Finish
50g/2oz/4 tbsp butter
30ml/2 tbsp oil
50g/2 oz/1 cup fresh breadcrumbs
15ml/1 tbsp snipped fresh chives
15ml/1 tbsp chopped fresh tarragon

1 Preheat the oven to 160°C/325°F/ Gas 3. Mix the flour and mustard powder together, then put on a plate.

2 Dip the rabbit joints in the flour mixture, reserve excess flour. Heat the butter and oil in a heavy flame-proof casserole, then brown the rabbit. Transfer to a plate. Stir in the onion and cook until soft.

3 Stir any reserved flour mixture into the casserole, cook for 1 minute, then stir in the beer, stock and vinegar. Bring to the boil and add the sugar and pepper. Simmer for 2 minutes.

4 Return the rabbit and any juices that have collected on the plate, to the casserole, cover tightly and cook in the oven for 1 hour.

5 Stir the prepared mustard and salt to taste into the casserole, cover again and cook for a further 15 minutes.

6 To finish, heat together the butter and oil in a frying pan and fry the breadcrumbs, stirring frequently, until golden, then stir in the herbs. Transfer the rabbit to a warmed serving dish, sprinkle over the breadcrumb mixture and serve hot.

TURKEY HOTPOT

INGREDIENTS

Serves 4
115g/4oz kidney beans, soaked
    overnight and drained
40g/1½oz/3 tbsp butter
2 herby pork sausages
450g/1 lb turkey casserole meat
3 leeks, sliced
2 carrots, finely chopped
4 tomatoes, chopped
10–15ml/2–3 tsp tomato purée (paste)
bouquet garni
400ml/14 fl oz/1⅔ cups chicken stock
salt and pepper

1 Cook the beans in boiling water for 40 minutes, then drain well.

2 Meanwhile, heat the butter in a flameproof casserole, then cook the sausages until browned and the fat runs. Drain on kitchen paper, stir the turkey into the casserole and cook until lightly browned all over, then transfer to a bowl using a slotted spoon. Stir the leeks and carrot into the casserole and brown lightly.

3 Add the tomatoes and tomato purée (paste) and simmer gently for about 5 minutes.

4 Chop the sausages and return to the casserole with the beans, turkey, bouquet garni, stock and seasoning. Cover and cook gently for about 1¼ hours, until the beans are tender and there is very little liquid.

CHICKEN AND MUSHROOM PIE

INGREDIENTS

Serves 6

15g/½oz dried porcini mushrooms
50g/2oz/4 tbsp butter
15g/½oz/2 tbsp plain flour
250ml/8fl oz/1 cup hot chicken stock
50ml/2fl oz/¼ cup single cream
    or milk
1 onion, coarsely chopped
2 carrots, sliced
2 celery sticks, coarsely chopped
50g/2oz fresh mushrooms, quartered
450g/1lb cooked chicken meat, cubed
50g/2oz fresh or frozen peas
salt and black pepper
beaten egg, to glaze

For the pastry

225g/8oz/2 cups plain flour
1.25ml/¼ tsp salt
115g/4oz/½ cup cold butter, cubed
65g/2½oz/⅓ cup white cooking fat,
    cubed
60–120ml/4–8 tablespoons iced water

2 Place the porcini mushrooms in a small bowl. Add hot water to cover and leave to soak for about 30 minutes, until soft. Lift out of the water with a slotted spoon to leave any grit behind and drain on kitchen paper. Discard the soaking water. Preheat the oven to 190°C/375°F/Gas 5.

3 Melt half of the butter in a heavy-based saucepan. Whisk in the flour and cook until bubbling, whisking constantly. Add the warm stock and cook over a medium heat, whisking, until the mixture boils. Cook for 2–3 minutes more, then whisk in the cream or milk. Season with salt and pepper and set aside.

5 Add the chicken mixture to the cream sauce and stir to mix. Taste for seasoning. Turn into a 2.5 litre/ 4 pint rectangular baking dish.

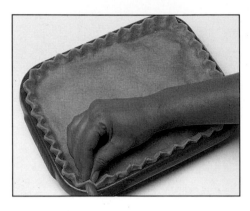

6 Roll out the dough to about a 3mm/⅛in thickness. Cut out a rectangle about 2.5cm/1in larger all around than the dish. Lay the rectangle of dough over the filling. Make a decorative edge by pushing the index finger of one hand between the thumb and index finger of the other.

7 Cut several slits in the pastry to allow steam to escape then brush the pastry with the beaten egg.

1 To make the pastry, sift the flour and salt into a bowl. With a pastry blender or two knives, cut in the butter and cooking fat until the mixture resembles breadcrumbs. Sprinkle with 90ml/6 tbsp iced water and mix until the dough holds together. If the dough is too crumbly, add a little more water, 15ml/1 tbsp at a time. Gather the dough into a ball and flatten into a round. Place in a sealed polythene bag and chill for at least 30 minutes.

4 Heat the remaining butter in a large non-stick frying pan until sizzling. Add the onion and carrots and cook for about 5 minutes, until softened. Add the celery and fresh mushrooms and cook for a further 5 minutes. Stir in the cooked chicken, peas and drained porcini mushrooms.

8 Press together the pastry trimmings and roll out again. Cut into thin strips and lay them over the pastry lid. Glaze again. If liked, roll small balls of dough and arrange them in the "windows" in the lattice.

9 Bake for about 30 minutes, until the pastry is browned. Serve the pie hot from the dish.

CHICKEN CHARTER PIE

Since this dish comes from Cornwall, typically cream is used in the filling.

────── INGREDIENTS ──────

Serves 4

50g/2oz/4 tbsp butter
4 chicken legs
1 onion, finely chopped
150ml/¼ pint/⅔ cup milk
150ml/¼ pint/⅔ cup soured (sour) cream
4 spring onions (scallions), quartered
20g/¾oz fresh parsley leaves, finely chopped
225g/8oz ready-made puff pastry
120ml/4 floz/½ cup double (heavy) cream
2 eggs, beaten, plus extra for glazing
salt and pepper

1. Melt the butter in a heavy-based, shallow pan, then brown the chicken legs. Transfer to a plate.

2. Add the chopped onion to the pan and cook until softened but not browned. Stir the milk, soured (sour) cream, spring onions (scallions), parsley and seasoning into the pan, bring to the boil, then simmer for a couple of minutes.

3. Return the chicken to the pan with any juices, then cover tightly and cook very gently for about 30 minutes. Transfer the chicken and sauce mixture to a 1.2 litre/2 pint/5 cup pie dish and leave to cool.

4. Meanwhile, roll out the pastry until about 2cm/¾in larger all round than the top of the pie dish. Leave the pastry to relax while the chicken is cooling.

5. Preheat the oven to 220°C/425°F/ Gas 7. Cut off a narrow strip around the edge of the pastry, then place the strip on the edge of the pie dish. Moisten the strip, then cover the dish with the pastry. Press the edges together.

6. Make a hole in the centre of the pastry and insert a small funnel of foil. Brush the pastry with beaten egg, then bake for 15–20 minutes.

7. Reduce the oven temperature to 180°C/350°F/Gas 4. Mix the cream and eggs, then pour into the pie through the funnel. Shake the pie to distribute the cream, then return to the oven for 5–10 minutes. Remove the pie from the oven and leave in a warm place for 5–10 minutes before serving, or cool completely if serving cold.

CHICKEN AND HAM PIE

This domed double-crust pie is suitable for a cold buffet, for picnics or any packed meals.

-----INGREDIENTS-----

Serves 8
400g/14oz ready-made shortcrust (pie) pastry
800g/1¾ lb chicken breast
350g/12oz uncooked gammon
about 60ml/4 tbsp double (heavy) cream
6 spring onions (scallions), finely chopped
15ml/1 tbsp chopped fresh tarragon
10ml/2 tsp chopped fresh thyme
grated rind and juice of ½ large lemon
5ml/1 tsp freshly ground mace
salt and pepper
beaten egg or milk, to glaze

1 Preheat the oven to 175°C/190°F/ Gas 5. Roll out one-third of the pastry and use it to line a 20cm/8in pie tin (pan) 5cm/2in deep. Place on a baking (cookie) sheet.

2 Mince (grind) 115g/4oz of the chicken with the gammon, then mix with the cream, spring onions (scallions), herbs, lemon rind, 15ml/1tbsp of the lemon juice and the seasoning to make a soft mixture; add more cream if necessary.

3 Cut the remaining chicken into 1cm/½ in pieces and mix with the remaining lemon juice, the mace and seasoning.

4 Make a layer of one-third of the gammon mixture in the pastry base, cover with half the chopped chicken, then add another layer of one-third of the gammon. Add all the remaining chicken followed by the remaining gammon.

5 Dampen the edges of the pastry base. Roll out the remaining pastry to make a lid for the pie.

6 Use the trimmings to make a lattice decoration. Make a small hole in the centre of the pie, brush the top with beaten egg or milk, then bake for about 20 minutes. Reduce the oven temperature to 160°C/325°F/Gas 3 and bake for a further 1-1¼ hours; cover the top with foil if the pastry becomes too brown. Transfer the pie to a wire rack and leave to cool.

CORONATION CHICKEN

INGREDIENTS

Serves 8
½ lemon
2.3kg/5 lb chicken
1 onion, quartered
1 carrot, quartered
large bouquet garni
8 black peppercorns, crushed
salt
watercress sprigs, to garnish

For The Sauce
1 small onion, chopped
15 g/½ oz/1 tbsp butter
15ml/1 tbsp curry paste
15ml/1 tbsp tomato purée (paste)
120ml/4 fl oz/½ cup red wine
bay leaf
juice of ½ lemon, or more to taste
10–15ml/2–3 tsp apricot jam
300ml/½ pint/1¼ cups mayonnaise
120ml/4 fl oz/½ cup whipping cream,
   whipped
salt and pepper

1 Put the lemon half in the chicken cavity, then place the chicken in a saucepan that it just fits. Add the vegetables, bouquet garni, peppercorns and salt.

2 Add sufficient water to come two-thirds of the way up the chicken, bring to the boil, then cover and cook gently for 1½ hours, until the chicken juices run clear.

3 Transfer the chicken to a large bowl, pour over the cooking liquid and leave to cool. When cold, skin and bone the chicken, then chop.

4 Make the sauce, cook the onion in the butter until soft. Add the curry paste, tomato purée (paste), wine, bay leaf and lemon juice, then cook for 10 minutes. Add the jam; sieve and cool.

5 Beat into the mayonnaise. Fold in the cream; add seasoning and lemon juice, then stir in the chicken.

DUCK WITH CUMBERLAND SAUCE

INGREDIENTS

Serves 4
4 duck portions
grated rind and juice of 1 lemon
grated rind and juice of 1 large orange
60ml/4 tbsp redcurrant jelly
60ml/4 tbsp port
pinch of ground mace or ginger
15ml/1 tbsp brandy
salt and pepper
orange slices, to garnish

1 Preheat the oven to 190°C/375°F/ Gas 5. Place a rack in a roasting tin (pan). Prick the duck portions all over, sprinkle with salt and pepper. Place the duck portions on the rack and cook in the oven for 45–50 minutes. until the duck skin is crisp and the juices run clear.

2 Meanwhile, simmer the lemon and orange juices and rinds together in a saucepan for 5 minutes.

3 Stir in the redcurrant jelly until melted, then stir in the port. Bring to the boil, add mace or ginger and seasoning to taste.

4 Transfer the duck to a serving plate; keep warm. Pour the fat from the roasting tin (pan), leaving the cooking juices. With the tin (pan) over a low heat, stir in the brandy, dislodging the sediment and bring to the boil. Stir in the port sauce and serve with the duck, garnished with orange slices.

DUCK BREASTS WITH BLACKBERRIES

If there isn't any blackberry, or bramble, jelly in your store-cupboard, you could substitute redcurrant jelly instead.

INGREDIENTS

Serves 4
4 duck breasts
finely grated rind and juice of 1 orange
30ml/2 tbsp blackberry (bramble) jelly
salt and black pepper

1 Heat a heavy-based frying pan and place the duck portions skin side down first. Fry for 3–4 minutes. Meanwhile, sprinkle the meat side with seasoning and the orange rind.

2 Turn the duck over and continue cooking for 3–4 minutes. Spread the skin side with some of the blackberry jelly while cooking, and pour the orange juice over the portions.

3 Spread a little more jelly over the duck breasts, then turn them over and cook for 1–2 minutes more, until just cooked, but still slightly pink in the middle. Serve the duck breasts with the glaze poured over, accompanied by new potatoes and a watercress and orange salad.

SPRING RABBIT CASSEROLE

If you have never tried rabbit before, you will find it very similar to chicken, but with just a slightly sweeter taste. You could replace the rabbit with chicken in this recipe, if you prefer – cook it in exactly the same way.

INGREDIENTS

Serves 4
15ml/1 tbsp sunflower oil
450g/1 lb boneless rabbit
4 rashers streaky bacon, rinded and chopped
2 leeks, sliced
4 spring onions, sliced
3 celery sticks, chopped
4 small carrots, sliced
300ml/½ pint/1¼ cups vegetable stock
10ml/2 tsp Dijon mustard
5ml/1 tsp grated lemon rind
45–60ml/3–4 tbsp crème fraîche
salt and black pepper
herby mashed potatoes, to serve

1 Heat the oil in a large flameproof casserole and fry the rabbit pieces until browned all over. Preheat the oven to 190°C/375°F/Gas 5.

2 Add the bacon and vegetables and toss over the heat for 1 minute. Add the stock, mustard, lemon rind and crème fraîche, and seasoning to taste, then bring to the boil.

3 Cover and cook for 35–40 minutes, or until the rabbit is tender (it should take no longer than chicken). Serve with herby mashed potatoes – creamed potatoes well flavoured and coloured with chopped fresh parsley and snipped chives.

RABBIT WITH PARSLEY SAUCE

INGREDIENTS

Serves 4
90ml/6 tbsp soy sauce
few drops of Tabasco sauce
5ml/1 tsp sweet paprika
5ml/1 tsp dried basil
1–1.5kg/2–3lb rabbit, cut into pieces
45ml/3 tbsp peanut or olive oil
75g/3oz/3/4 cup plain flour
1 large onion, finely sliced
250ml/8fl oz/1 cup dry white wine
250ml/8fl oz/1 cup chicken stock
2 cloves garlic, finely chopped
60ml/4 tbsp fresh chopped parsley
salt and white pepper
mashed potatoes or rice, to serve
fresh parsley sprigs, to garnish

1 Combine the soy sauce, Tabasco sauce, white pepper, paprika, and basil in a medium-sized bowl. Add the rabbit pieces and turn them over in the mixture so they are coated thoroughly. Let marinate at least 1 hour.

2 Heat the oil in a flameproof casserole. Coat the rabbit pieces lightly in the flour, shaking off the excess. Brown the rabbit pieces in the hot oil for about 5–6 minutes, turning them frequently. Remove the rabbit pieces with a slotted spoon and set aside on a plate or dish. Preheat the oven to 180°C/350°F/Gas 4.

3 Add the onion to the casserole and cook over a low heat for 8–10 minutes, until softened. Increase the heat, add the wine, and stir well to mix in all the cooking juices.

4 Return the rabbit and any juices to the casserole. Add the stock, garlic, parsley and salt. Mix well and turn the rabbit to coat with the sauce. Cover and place in the oven. Cook for about 1 hour, until the rabbit is tender, stirring occasionally. Serve garnished with parsley sprigs and accompanied by mashed potatoes or rice.

GUINEA FOWL WITH CIDER AND APPLES

Guinea fowl are farmed, so they are available quite frequently in supermarkets, usually fresh. Their flavour is reminiscent of an old-fashioned chicken – not really gamey, but they do have slightly darker meat.

INGREDIENTS

Serves 4–6
1.75kg/4–4½ lb guinea fowl
1 onion, halved
3 celery sticks
3 bay leaves
little butter
300ml/½ pint/1¼ cups dry cider
150ml/¼ pint/⅔ cup chicken stock
2 small apples, peeled and sliced
60ml/4 tbsp thick double cream
few sage leaves
30ml/2 tbsp chopped fresh parsley
salt and black pepper

1 If the guinea fowl is packed with its giblets, put them in a pan with water to cover, half the onion, a stick of celery, a bay leaf and seasoning. Simmer for 30 minutes, or until you have about 150ml/¼ pint/⅔ cup well-flavoured stock.

2 Preheat the oven to 190°C/375°F/ Gas 5. Wash and wipe dry the bird and place the remaining onion half and a knob of butter inside the body cavity. Place in a roasting dish, sprinkle with seasoning to taste, and dot with a few knobs of butter.

3 Pour the cider and chicken stock into the dish and cover with a lid or foil. Bake for 25 minutes per 450g/1 lb, basting occasionally.

4 Uncover for the last 20 minutes, baste well again and add the prepared apples and the celery, sliced. When the guinea fowl is cooked, transfer it to a warm serving dish and keep warm. Remove the apples and celery with a slotted spoon and set aside.

5 Boil the liquid rapidly to reduce to about 150ml/¼ pint/⅔ cup. Stir in the cream, seasoning to taste and the sage leaves, and cook for a few minutes more to reduce slightly. Return the apples to this pan with the parsley and warm through, then serve with or around the bird.

POT-ROAST OF VENISON

INGREDIENTS

Serves 4–5

1.75kg/4–4½ lb boned joint of
   venison
75ml/5 tbsp oil
4 cloves
8 black peppercorns, lightly crushed
12 juniper berries, lightly crushed
250ml/8 fl oz/1 cup full-bodied red
   wine
115g/4oz lightly smoked streaky
   bacon, chopped
2 onions, finely chopped
2 carrots, chopped
150g/5oz large mushrooms, sliced
15ml/1 tbsp plain (all-purpose) flour
250ml/8 fl oz/1 cup veal stock
30ml/2 tbsp redcurrant jelly
salt and pepper

1 Put the venison in a bowl, add half the oil, the spices and wine, cover and leave in a cool place for 24 hours, turning the meat occasionally.

2 Preheat the oven to 160°C/325°F/ Gas 3. Remove the venison from the bowl and pat dry. Reserve the marinade. Heat the remaining oil in a shallow pan, then brown the venison evenly. Transfer to a plate.

3 Stir the bacon, onions, carrots and mushrooms into the pan and cook for about 5 minutes. Stir in the flour and cook for 2 minutes, then remove from the heat and stir in the marinade, stock, redcurrant jelly and seasoning. Return to the heat, bring to the boil, stirring, then simmer for 2–3 minutes.

4 Transfer the venison and sauce to a casserole, cover and cook in the oven, turning the joint occasionally, for about 3 hours, until tender.

PHEASANT WITH MUSHROOMS

INGREDIENTS

Serves 4

1 pheasant, jointed
250ml/8 fl oz/1 cup red wine
45ml/3 tbsp oil
60ml/4 tbsp Spanish sherry vinegar
1 large onion, chopped
2 slices smoked bacon, cut into strips
350g/12oz chestnut (brown)
   mushrooms, sliced
3 anchovy fillets, soaked for 10
   minutes and drained
350ml/12 fl oz/1½ cups game, veal or
   chicken stock
bouquet garni
salt and pepper

1 Place the pheasant in a dish, add the wine, half the oil and half the vinegar, and scatter over half the onion. Season, then cover and leave in a cool place for 8–12 hours, turning the pheasant occasionally.

2 Preheat the oven to 160°C/325°F/ Gas 3. Lift the pheasant from the dish, pat dry. Reserve the marinade.

3 Heat the remaining oil in a flame-proof casserole, then brown the pheasant joints. Transfer to a plate.

4 Add the bacon and remaining onion to the casserole and cook until the onion is soft. Stir in the mushrooms and cook for about 3 minutes.

5 Stir in the anchovies and remaining vinegar, boil until reduced. Add the marinade, cook for 2 minutes, then add the stock and bouquet garni. Return the pheasant to the casserole, cover and bake for about 1½ hours. Transfer the pheasant to a serving dish. Boil the cooking juices to reduce. Discard the bouquet garni. Pour over the pheasant and serve at once.

FISH AND SEAFOOD

Britain is surrounded by good sea-fishing waters and has an abundance of rivers, streams and lakes teeming with freshwater fish. Yet the British eat relatively little fish, and traditional recipes feature surprisingly few varieties. Consumption in the past was far greater, but declined after the abolition of compulsory fish days, which once banned meat-eating on sometimes as many as three days a week. British favourites include recipes like Mackerel With Gooseberry Sauce and Herrings In Oatmeal With Mustard Sauce. In other recipes, plainly cooked, succulent fish is accompanied by classic sauces for instance, Haddock With Parsley Sauce and Cod With Caper Sauce. Besides warming casseroles and pies, there are homely dishes like Fish Cakes, and party pieces such as Salmon with Cucumber Sauce.

BAKED TROUT WITH OLIVES

INGREDIENTS

Serves 4

50g/2oz/1 cup fresh wholemeal breadcrumbs
25g/1oz chopped ham
50g/2oz/½ cup finely chopped black
olives
1 garlic clove, crushed
1 egg yolk
4 trout (about 175g/6oz each)
120ml/4fl oz/¼ cup dry martini
25g/1oz/2 tbsp butter
15g/½oz/1 tbsp plain flour
150ml/¼ pint/⅔ cup fish stock
45–60ml/3–4 tbsp single cream
salt and black pepper

1 Preheat the oven to 180°C/350°F/
Gas 4. Mix the breadcrumbs, ham,
olives, garlic, egg yolk and seasoning
together. Pack into the trout and place
each one on a sheet of greased foil.

2 Pour 15ml/1 tbsp dry martini over
each one, dot with half of the butter
and wrap up closely. Bake for 20–25
minutes, or until tender.

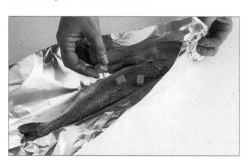

3 Melt the remaining butter in a small
pan and blend in the flour. Whisk in
the remaining martini, the stock and
the juices which have come out of the
fish during cooking and cook for 1–2
minutes until thickened.

4 Stir in the cream, then season the
sauce to taste and pour a little over
each fish before serving hot.

SALMON CAKES WITH BUTTER SAUCE

Salmon fish cakes make a real
treat for supper or a leisurely
breakfast at the weekend. You
could use any small tail pieces
which are on special offer.

INGREDIENTS

Makes 6

225g/8oz tail piece of salmon, cooked
30ml/2 tbsp chopped fresh parsley
2 spring onions, trimmed and chopped
grated rind and juice of ½ lemon
225g/8oz mashed potato (not too soft)
1 egg, beaten
50g/2oz/1 cup fresh white breadcrumbs
75g/3oz/6 tbsp butter

1 Remove all the skin and bones from
the fish and mash or flake it well.
Add the parsley, onions and 5ml/1 tsp
of the lemon rind and season with salt
and black pepper.

2 Gently work in the potato and then
shape into six rounds, triangles or
croquettes. Chill for 20 minutes.

3 Coat well in egg and then the breadcrumbs. Grill gently for 5 minutes
each side, or until golden, or fry in butter and oil.

4 To make the butter sauce, melt the
butter, whisk in the remaining
lemon rind, the lemon juice, 15–30ml/
1–2 tbsp water and seasoning to taste.
Simmer for a few minutes and serve
with the hot fish cakes.

HERRINGS IN OATMEAL WITH MUSTARD

──── INGREDIENTS ────

Serves 4

about 15ml/1 tbsp Dijon mustard
about 7.5ml/1½ tsp tarragon vinegar
175ml/6 fl oz/¾ cup thick mayonnaise
4 herrings, about 225g/8oz each
1 lemon, halved
115g/4oz/¾ cup medium oatmeal
salt and pepper

1 Beat mustard and vinegar to taste into the mayonnaise. Chill lightly.

2 Place one fish at a time on a board, cut side down and opened out. Press gently along the backbone with your thumbs. Turn over the fish and carefully lift away the backbone.

3 Squeeze lemon juice over both sides of the fish, then season with salt and pepper. Fold the fish in half, skin side outwards.

4 Preheat a grill (broiler) until fairly hot. Place the oatmeal on a plate, then coat each herring evenly in the oatmeal, pressing it in gently.

5 Place the herrings on a grill (broiler) rack and grill (broil) the fish for 3–4 minutes on each side, until the skin is golden brown and crisp and the flesh flakes easily. Serve hot with the mustard sauce, served separately.

FISH AND CHIPS

──── INGREDIENTS ────

Serves 4

115g/4oz/1 cup self-raising (self-rising)
  flour
150ml/¼ pint/⅔ cup water
675g/1½ lb potatoes
675g/1½ lb piece skinned cod fillet, cut
  into four pieces
oil, for deep frying
salt and pepper
lemon wedges, to serve

1 Stir the flour and salt together in a bowl, then form a well in the centre. Gradually pour in the water, whisking in the flour to make a smooth batter. Leave for 30 minutes.

2 Cut the potatoes into strips about 1cm/½ in wide and 5cm/2 in long, using a sharp knife. Place the potatoes in a colander and rinse them in cold water, then drain and dry well.

3 Heat the oil in a deep-fat fryer or large heavy pan to 150°C/300°F. Using the wire basket, lower the potatoes in batches into the oil and cook for 5–6 minutes, shaking the basket occasionally until the potatoes are soft but not browned. Remove the chips from the oil and drain thoroughly on kitchen paper.

4 Heat the oil in the fryer to 190°C/375°F. Season the fish. Stir the batter, then dip the pieces of fish in turn into it, allowing the excess to drain off.

5 Working in two batches if necessary, lower the fish into the oil and fry for 6–8 minutes, until crisp and brown. Drain the fish on kitchen paper and keep warm.

6 Add the chips in batches to the oil and cook for 2–3 minutes, until brown and crisp. Keep hot. Sprinkle with salt and serve with the fish, accompanied by lemon wedges.

HADDOCK WITH PARSLEY SAUCE

As the fish has to be kept warm while the sauce is made, take care not to overcook it.

INGREDIENTS

Serves 4
4 haddock fillets, about 175g/6oz each
50g/2oz/4 tbsp butter
150ml ¼ pint/⅔ cup milk
150ml/¼ pint/⅔ cup fish stock
1 bay leaf
20ml/4 tsp plain (all-purpose) flour
60ml/4 tbsp cream
1 egg yolk
45ml/3 tbsp chopped fresh parsley
grated rind and juice of ½ lemon
salt and pepper

1 Place the fish in a frying pan, add half the butter, the milk, fish stock, bay leaf and seasoning, and heat over a low-medium heat to simmering point. Lower the heat, cover the pan and poach the fish for 10–15 minutes, depending on the thickness of the fillets, until the fish is tender and the flesh just begins to flake.

2 Transfer the fish to a warmed serving plate, cover the fish and keep warm while you make the sauce. Return the cooking liquid to the heat and bring to the boil, stirring. Simmer for about 4 minutes, then remove and discard the bay leaf.

3 Melt the remaining butter in a saucepan, stir in the flour and cook, stirring, for 1 minute. Remove from the heat and gradually stir in the fish cooking liquid. Return to the heat and bring to the boil, stirring. Simmer for about 4 minutes, stirring frequently. Discard the bay leaf.

4 Remove the pan from the heat, blend the cream into the egg yolk, then stir into the sauce with the parsley. Reheat gently, stirring, for a few minutes; do not allow to boil.

5 Remove from the heat and add the lemon juice and rind, and season to taste. Pour into a warmed sauceboat and serve with the fish.

MACKEREL WITH GOOSEBERRY SAUCE

Gooseberries and mackerel are a classic combination; the tart flavour of the sauce offsets the richness of the fish.

INGREDIENTS

Serves 4
15g/½ oz/1 tbsp butter
225g/8oz gooseberries, topped and tailed
4 fresh mackerel, about 350g/12oz each, cleaned
1 egg, beaten
pinch of ground mace or ginger, or a few drops of orange flower water (optional)
salt and pepper
flat leaf parsley, to garnish

1 Melt the butter in a saucepan, add the gooseberries, then cover and cook over a low heat, shaking the pan until the gooseberries are just tender.

2 Meanwhile, preheat the grill (broiler). Season the fish inside and out with salt and black pepper.

3 Cut 2 or 3 slashes in the skin on both sides of each mackerel, then grill (broil) for 15–20 minutes until cooked, turning once.

> COOK'S TIP
> For the best flavour, look for triple strength orange flower water, which can be obtained from chemists and good food shops.

4 Purée the gooseberries with the egg in a food processor or blender, or mash the gooseberries thoroughly in a bowl with the egg. Press the gooseberry mixture through a sieve (strainer).

5 Return the gooseberry mixture to the pan and reheat gently, stirring, but do not allow to boil. Add the mace, ginger or orange flower water, if using, and seasoning to taste. Serve hot with the mackerel.

BAKED HADDOCK WITH TOMATOES

INGREDIENTS

Serves 6

1kg/2¼lb thick haddock fillets,
skinned
45ml/3 tbsp olive oil
5ml/1 tsp drained capers, chopped
2 garlic cloves, chopped
2 ripe tomatoes, peeled, seeded, and
finely diced
30ml/2 tbsp chopped fresh basil
250ml/8fl oz/1 cup dry white wine
salt and black pepper
sprigs of basil, to garnish
salad leaves, to serve

1 Preheat the oven to 200°C/400°F/
Gas 6. Arrange the fillets in an
oiled baking dish. Brush with oil.

2 Mix together the capers, garlic,
tomatoes and basil. Season well.

3 Spoon the tomato mixture over the
fish and pour in the wine. Bake for
15–20 minutes, until the fish is cooked
and opaque in the centre. Garnish each
serving with sprigs of basil and serve
with salad leaves.

LEMON SOLE WITH CRAB

INGREDIENTS

Serves 6

50g/2oz/4 tbsp butter or margarine
45ml/3 tbsp plain flour
250ml/8fl oz/1 cup fish stock, or 175ml/
6fl oz/¾ cup fish stock mixed with
45ml/3 tbsp dry white wine
250ml/8fl oz/1 cup milk
1 bay leaf
6 lemon sole fillets, halved lengthways
200g/7oz can crab meat, drained
90ml/6 tbsp freshly grated
Parmesan cheese
salt and black pepper
flat leaf parsley, to garnish
cherry tomatoes and lettuce leaves,
to serve

1 Preheat the oven to 220°C/425°F/
Gas 7 and butter a large shallow
baking dish.

> **VARIATIONS**
> Other flat white fish, such as
> plaice, can be substituted for the
> lemon sole, if you prefer.

2 Melt the butter or margarine in a
medium-sized, heavy-based
saucepan over a medium heat. Stir in
the flour and cook for 2–3 minutes.

3 Pour in the fish stock (or the mixed
fish stock and wine) together with
the milk and whisk until smooth.

4 Add the bay leaf. Raise the heat to
high and bring to the boil. Cook for
3–4 minutes. Then remove the sauce
from the heat and add salt to taste.
Keep warm while preparing the fish.

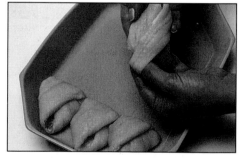

5 Twist each fish fillet to form a neat
cone shape and arrange in the
prepared baking dish. Sprinkle the crab
meat over the fish. Pour the hot sauce
evenly over the top and sprinkle with
the Parmesan cheese.

6 Bake for 10–12 minutes, until the
top is golden brown and the fish is
cooked. Serve garnished with flat leaf
parsley and accompanied by cherry
tomatoes and lettuce leaves.

OMELETTE ARNOLD BENNETT

After creating this dish while staying at London's Savoy Hotel, the author, Arnold Bennett, insisted that chefs around the world, wherever he stayed, cooked it for him.

INGREDIENTS

Serves 2
175g/6oz smoked haddock fillet, poached and drained
50g/2 oz/4 tbsp butter, diced
175ml/6 fl oz/¾ cup whipping or double (heavy) cream
4 eggs, separated
65g/2½ oz/generous ½ cup grated mature Cheddar cheese
salt and pepper

1 Discard the haddock skin and any bones and flake the flesh.

2 Melt half the butter in 60ml/4 tbsp cream in a fairly small non-stick saucepan, then lightly stir in the fish. Cover, remove from the heat and leave the mixture to cool.

3 Stir together the egg yolks, 15ml/1 tbsp cream and pepper, then lightly stir in the fish mixture. In a separate bowl, mix together the cheese and the remaining cream.

4 Whisk the egg whites until stiff, then fold into the fish mixture.

5 Heat the remaining butter in an omelette pan, add the fish mixture and cook until browned underneath. Pour over the cheese mixture, then grill (broil) until golden and bubbling.

FISH CAKES

For extra-special fish cakes, you could use cooked fresh – or drained, canned – salmon.

INGREDIENTS

Serves 4
450g/1 lb cooked, mashed potatoes
450g/1 lb cooked mixed white and smoked fish such as haddock or cod, flaked
25g/1oz/2 tbsp butter, diced
45ml/3 tbsp chopped fresh parsley
1 egg, separated
1 egg, beaten
about 50g/2oz/1 cup fine breadcrumbs made with stale bread
pepper
vegetable oil, for frying

1 Place the potatoes in a bowl and beat in the fish, butter, parsley and egg yolk. Season with pepper.

2 Divide the fish mixture into eight equal portions, then, with floured hands, form each into a flat cake.

3 Beat the remaining egg white with the whole egg. Dip each fish cake in the beaten egg, then in breadcrumbs.

4 Heat the oil in a frying pan, then fry the fish cakes for about 3–5 minutes on each side, until crisp and golden. Drain on kitchen paper and serve hot with a crisp salad.

FISHERMAN'S CASSEROLE

INGREDIENTS

Serves 4–6

*450g/1 lb mixed firm fish fillets such
    as cod, haddock and monkfish*
50g/2oz/4 tbsp butter
1 onion, sliced
1 celery stick, sliced
350g/12oz potatoes, cut into chunks
750ml/1¼ pints/3⅔ cups fish stock
bouquet garni
150g/5oz frozen broad (fava) beans
300ml/½ pint/1¼ cups milk
115g/4oz peeled prawns (shrimp)
8 shelled (shucked) mussels
salt and pepper
chopped parsley, to garnish

1 Skin the fish and cut the flesh into bite-sized chunks using a large sharp knife. Heat the butter in a saucepan, then fry the onion and celery until softened but not coloured. Stir the chunks of potato into the pan and cook for 1–2 minutes.

2 Add the stock and bouquet garni. Bring to the boil, cover and simmer for 20 minutes, until tender.

3 Add the fish, beans and milk and simmer for 6 minutes, until the fish flakes. Add the prawns (shrimp), mussels and seasoning and warm through. Sprinkle with parsley to serve.

FISH PIE

INGREDIENTS

Serves 4

400ml/14 fl oz/1¾ cups milk
1 bay leaf
¼ onion, sliced
450g/1 lb haddock or cod fillet
225g/8oz smoked haddock fillet
3 hard-boiled eggs, chopped
65g/2½oz/5 tbsp butter
25g/1oz/2 tbsp plain (all-purpose) flour
115g/4oz/1 cup peas
75g/3oz prawns (shrimp) (optional)
30ml/2 tbsp chopped fresh parsley
lemon juice, to taste
500g/1¼ lb potatoes, cooked
60ml/4 tbsp hot milk
60ml/4 tbsp grated Cheddar cheese
salt and pepper

1 Place 350ml/12 fl oz/1½ cups milk, the bay leaf and onion in a saucepan, then add the fish. Cover and poach for 8–10 minutes. Strain and reserve the milk. Flake the fish into a pie dish, discarding the skin and any bones. Add the eggs.

2 Melt 25g/1 oz/2 tbsp butter in a saucepan, stir in the flour and cook gently for 1 minute, stirring. Remove from the heat and stir in the reserved milk. Return to the heat and bring to the boil, stirring. Simmer the sauce for 4 minutes, stirring all the time. Remove from the heat and stir in the peas and prawns (shrimp).

3 Add the parsley, lemon juice and seasoning to taste. Pour the sauce over the fish and eggs and carefully mix together.

4 Preheat the oven to 180°C/350°F/ Gas 4. Gently heat the remaining butter in the remaining milk in a small saucepan, then beat into the potato. Spoon evenly over the fish and fork up the surface.

5 Sprinkle the cheese over the pie, then bake for 25–30 minutes, until golden. Serve piping hot.

HERRINGS WITH WALNUT STUFFING

Ask the fishmonger to prepare the fish – mackerel can be used if herrings are not available.

INGREDIENTS

Serves 4

25g/1oz/2 tbsp butter
1 onion, finely chopped
50g/2oz/6 tbsp fresh white breadcrumbs
50g/2oz/½ cup shelled walnuts, toasted and chopped
finely grated rind of ½ lemon
15ml/1 tbsp lemon juice
10ml/2 tsp wholegrain mustard
45ml/3 tbsp mixed chopped fresh herbs, such as sage, thyme and parsley
4 herrings, about 275g/10oz each, without heads and tails, boned
salt and black pepper
lemon wedges and flat leaf parsley sprigs, to garnish

1 Preheat the oven to 190°C/375°F/ Gas 5. Melt the butter in a frying pan and fry the onion for about 10 minutes until golden.

2 Stir in the breadcrumbs, chopped walnuts, lemon rind and juice, mustard and herbs. Mix together, then season with salt and pepper to taste.

3 Open out the herring fillets and divide the stuffing among them. Fold the herrings back in half and slash the skin several times on each side.

4 Arrange the herrings in a lightly greased shallow baking tin and bake for 20–25 minutes. Serve hot, garnished with lemon wedges and parsley sprigs.

TROUT WITH MUSHROOM SAUCE

INGREDIENTS

Serves 4

8 pink trout fillets
seasoned plain flour
75g/3oz/6 tbsp butter
1 garlic clove, chopped
10ml/2 tsp chopped fresh sage
350g/12oz mixed wild or cultivated mushrooms
90ml/6 tbsp dry white wine
250ml/8fl oz/1 cup double cream
salt and black pepper

> **COOK'S TIP**
> Use a large sharp knife to ease the skin from the trout fillets, then pull out any bones from the flesh – a pair of tweezers makes easy work of this fiddly task!

1 Remove the skin from the trout fillets, then carefully remove any bones.

2 Lightly dust the trout fillets on both sides in the seasoned flour, shaking off any excess.

3 Melt the butter in a large frying pan, add the trout fillets and fry gently over a moderate heat for 4–5 minutes, turning once. Remove from the pan and keep warm.

4 Add the garlic, sage and mushrooms to the pan and fry until softened.

5 Pour in the wine and boil briskly to allow the alcohol to evaporate. Stir in the cream and seasoning.

6 Serve the trout fillets on warmed plates with the sauce spooned over. Garnish with a few fresh sage sprigs, if you have them.

MACKEREL WITH MUSTARD AND LEMON

Mackerel must be really fresh to be enjoyed. Look for bright, firm-looking fish.

INGREDIENTS

Serves 4

*4 fresh mackerel, about 275g/10oz
 each, gutted and cleaned*
175–225g/6–8oz young spinach leaves

For the mustard and lemon butter
115g/4oz/½ cup butter, melted
30ml/2 tbsp wholegrain mustard
grated rind of 1 lemon
30ml/2 tbsp lemon juice
45ml/3 tbsp chopped fresh parsley
salt and black pepper

1 To prepare each mackerel, cut off the heads just behind the gills, using a sharp knife, then cut along the belly so that the fish can be opened out flat.

2 Place the fish on a board, skin-side up, and, with the heel of your hand, press along the backbone to loosen it.

3 Turn the fish the right way up and pull the bone away from the flesh. Remove the tail and cut each fish in half lengthways. Wash and pat dry.

4 Score the skin three or four times, then season the fish. To make the mustard and lemon butter, mix together the melted butter, mustard, lemon rind and juice, parsley and seasoning. Place the mackerel on a grill rack. Brush a little of the butter over the mackerel and grill for 5 minutes each side, basting occasionally, until cooked through.

5 Arrange the spinach leaves in the centre of four large plates. Place the mackerel on top. Heat the remaining butter in a small pan until sizzling and pour over the mackerel. Serve at once.

SCOTTISH SALMON WITH HERB BUTTER

INGREDIENTS

Serves 4

50g/2oz/4 tbsp butter, softened
finely grated rind of ½ small lemon
15ml/1 tbsp lemon juice
15ml/1 tbsp chopped fresh dill
4 salmon steaks
2 lemon slices, halved
4 fresh dill sprigs
salt and black pepper

1 Place the butter, lemon rind, lemon juice, chopped dill and seasoning in a small bowl and mix together with a fork until blended.

2 Spoon the butter on to a piece of greaseproof paper and roll up, smoothing with your hands into a sausage shape. Twist the ends tightly, wrap in clear film and pop in the freezer for 20 minutes, until firm.

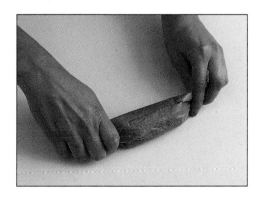

COOK'S TIP
Other fresh herbs could be used to flavour the butter – try mint, fennel fronds, lemon balm, parsley or oregano instead of the dill.

3 Meanwhile, preheat the oven to 190°C/375°F/Gas 5. Cut out four squares of foil big enough to encase the salmon steaks and grease lightly. Place a salmon steak in the centre of each one.

4 Remove the butter from the freezer and slice into eight rounds. Place two rounds on top of each salmon steak with a halved lemon slice in the centre and a sprig of dill on top. Lift up the edges of the foil and crinkle them together until well sealed.

5 Lift the parcels on to a baking sheet and bake for about 20 minutes. Remove from the oven and place the unopened parcels on warmed plates. Open the parcels and slide the contents on to the plates with the juices.

HALIBUT WITH FENNEL AND ORANGE

INGREDIENTS

Serves 4
1 fennel bulb, thinly sliced
grated rind and juice of 1 orange
150ml/ ¼ pint/⅔ cup dry white wine
4 halibut steaks, about 200g/7oz each
50g/2oz/4 tbsp butter
salt and pepper
fennel fronds, to garnish

1 Preheat the oven to 180°C/350°F/
Gas 4. Butter a shallow baking dish.

2 Add the fennel to a saucepan of
boiling water, return to the boil and
boil for 4–6 minutes, until just tender.

3 Meanwhile, cook the orange rind,
juice and wine until reduced by half.

4 Drain the fennel well, then spread
in the baking dish and season.
Arrange the halibut on the fennel,
season, dot with butter, then pour over
the reduced orange and wine.

5 Cover and bake for about 20
minutes, until the flesh flakes. Serve
garnished with fennel fronds.

SALMON WITH CUCUMBER SAUCE

INGREDIENTS

Serves 6–8
1.8 kg/4 lb salmon, gutted and scaled
melted butter, for brushing
3 parsley or thyme sprigs
½ lemon, halved
1 large cucumber, peeled
25g/1oz/2 tbsp butter
115ml/4 fl oz/ ½ cup dry white wine
3 tbsp finely chopped fresh dill (dill-
   weed)
60ml/4 tbsp soured (sour) cream
salt and pepper

1 Preheat the oven to 220°C/425°F/
Gas 7. Season the salmon and brush
inside and out with melted butter.
Place the herbs and lemon in the cavity.

2 Wrap the salmon in foil, folding the
edges together securely, then bake
for 15 minutes. Remove the fish from
the oven and leave in the foil for 1 hour,
then remove the skin from the salmon.

3 Meanwhile, halve the cucumber
lengthways, scoop out the seeds,
then dice the flesh.

4 Place the cucumber in a colander,
toss lightly with salt, leave for
about 30 minutes to drain , then rinse
well and pat dry.

5 Heat the butter in a small saucepan,
add the cucumber and cook for
about 2 minutes, until translucent but
not soft. Add the wine to the pan and
boil briskly until the cucumber is dry.

6 Stir the dill (dillweed) and soured
(sour) cream into the cucumber.
Season to taste and serve immediately
with the salmon.

COD WITH CAPER SAUCE

The quick and easy sauce with a slightly sharp and 'nutty' flavour is a very effective way of enhancing the fish.

INGREDIENTS

Serves 4
4 cod steaks, about 175g/6oz each
115g/4 oz/½ cup butter
15ml/1 tbsp vinegar from the caper jar
15ml/1 tbsp small capers
15ml/1 tbsp chopped fresh parsley
salt and pepper
tarragon sprigs, to garnish

1 Preheat the grill (broiler). Season the cod. Melt 25g/1oz/2 tbsp of the butter, then brush some over one side of each piece of cod.

2 Grill (broil) the cod for about 6 minutes, turn the fish over, brush with melted butter and cook for a further 5–6 minutes or until the fish flakes easily.

3 Meanwhile, heat the remaining butter until it turns golden brown, then add the vinegar followed by the capers and stir well.

4 Pour the vinegar, butter and capers over the fish, sprinkle with parsley and garnish with the tarragon sprigs.

COOK'S TIP
Thick tail fillets of cod or haddock could be used in place of the cod steaks, if you prefer.

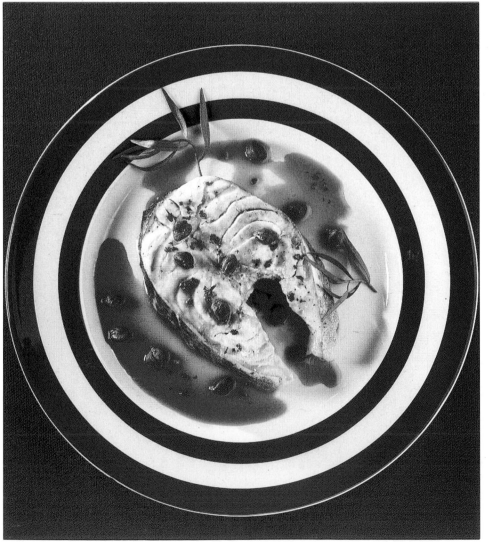

STUFFED PLAICE FILLETS

------ INGREDIENTS ------

Serves 4

8 plaice fillets, skinned
115g/4oz/ ½ cup firm cottage cheese,
   drained
few drops Tabasco sauce
grated rind and juice of 1 lemon
90g/3½ oz peeled prawns (shrimp),
   finely chopped
1kg/2 lb spinach, stalks removed
45ml/3 tbsp single (light) cream
25g/1oz/2 tbsp butter, finely diced
pinch of freshly grated nutmeg
30ml/2 tbsp finely grated mature
   Cheddar cheese
salt and pepper

1 Preheat the oven to 180°C/350°F/
Gas 4. Season the fillets of fish and
place skinned-side up on a plate or
chopping board.

2 Mash the cheese with the Tabasco
and the lemon rind and juice. Mix
in the prawns (shrimp).

3 Spread the cheese mixture on the
fillets and roll them up neatly.
Secure with wooden cocktail sticks
(toothpicks).

4 Wash but do not dry the spinach,
place it in a saucepan with just the
water left on the leaves and cook until
no surplus liquid is visible. Tip the
spinach into a sieve (strainer) and press
firmly to expel surplus liquid.

5 Gently heat together the cream,
butter, nutmeg, seasoning and
spinach, then spread in a shallow baking dish just large enough to hold the
fish in a single layer. Put the fish rolls
in the dish and sprinkle them with
cheese. Cover the dish with foil and
bake for 20–25 minutes, until the fish
is tender.

COOK'S TIP
You can use fillets of lemon sole
instead of plaice, if you like.

VEGETABLES AND SALADS

The most well-to-do considered the consumption of meat, poultry, game and fish an indication of wealth and relegated vegetables to a secondary role. Yet vegetables played an important role in the diet of most of the population and cookery writers of the eighteenth century recorded many excellent ways of cooking a surprisingly large variety of vegetables that retained their taste, texture and value. In the 1920s it was said that 'The English have only three vegetables and two of them are cabbage'. Happily, attitudes have changed. Mouth-watering dishes include Lemony Carrots, Parsnips with Almonds and Turnips with Orange; there are classic salads, and even the clichéd cabbage becomes a star turn in Braised Red Cabbage and Cabbage with Bacon.

BEANS WITH PARSLEY SAUCE

If you grow the herb summer savory, or know someone who does, substitute this for the parsley, as it has a special affinity with broad (fava) beans.

─── INGREDIENTS ───

Serves 4

20g/¾oz/1½ tbsp butter
1–1.12 kg/2–2½ lb fresh broad (fava)
  beans, shelled
1 large parsley sprig
150ml/¼ pint/⅔ cup double (heavy) or
  whipping cream
3 egg yolks
few drops of lemon juice
salt and pepper
chopped parsley, to garnish

1 Melt the butter in a saucepan, stir in the beans for 2–3 minutes, then add the parsley, seasoning and enough water barely to cover the beans.

2 Cover the pan tightly, bring just to the boil, then immediately lower the heat and cook very gently, shaking the pan occasionally, for 15–20 minutes until the beans are tender and there is no free liquid. Remove the pan from the heat and leave to cool slightly.

3 Mix the cream with the egg yolks, then stir into the beans. Reheat gently, stirring, until the sauce coats the back of the spoon; do not boil.

4 Add a few drops of lemon juice and garnish with chopped parsley.

BRAISED LETTUCE AND PEAS

Slow, gentle cooking is ideal for older garden peas, but it is also effective with young ones. Serve with lamb or chicken.

─── INGREDIENTS ───

Serves 4

25g/1oz/2 tbsp butter
300g/10oz/2 cups shelled fresh peas
8 spring onions (scallions)
1 small firm lettuce, shredded
15ml/1 tbsp chopped fresh parsley
60ml/4 tbsp water
sugar (optional)
salt and pepper

1 Mix the butter, peas, spring onions (scallions), lettuce, parsley, seasoning and water together in a heavy-based saucepan.

2 Cover the pan very tightly and cook very gently for 20–25 minutes, shaking the pan occasionally, until the peas are tender. Should the pan become dry, add just a little water.

3 Taste the peas for seasoning and add a little sugar, if necessary.

BRUSSELS SPROUTS WITH CHESTNUTS

You really have to wait until late autumn or early winter to enjoy this dish, because fresh chestnuts are one of the few foods that are still seasonal.

──────INGREDIENTS──────

350g/12oz fresh chestnuts
300ml/½ pint/1¼ cups chicken or
  vegetable stock (optional)
5ml/1 tsp sugar
675g/1½ lb Brussels sprouts
50g/2oz/4 tbsp butter
115g/4oz streaky bacon, cut into strips

1 Cut a cross in the pointed end of each chestnut, then cook in boiling water for 5–10 minutes.

2 Drain the chestnuts, then peel off both the tough outer skin and the finer inner one. Return the chestnuts to the pan, add the stock if using, or water, and sugar and simmer gently for 30–35 minutes, until the chestnuts are tender, then drain thoroughly.

3 Meanwhile, cook the sprouts in boiling salted water for 8–10 minutes, until tender, then drain well.

4 Melt the butter, add the bacon, cook until becoming crisp, then stir in the chestnuts for 2–3 minutes. Add the sprouts and toss together.

BRAISED CELERY

The leaves from the celery can be used as a herb, to flavour soups and casseroles.

──────INGREDIENTS──────

Serves 4
40g/1½ oz/3 tbsp butter
2 slices bacon, chopped
1 small onion, finely chopped
1 carrot, finely chopped
1 head of celery, cut into 2.5cm/1in
  lengths
175ml/6 fl oz/¾ cup chicken or
  vegetable stock
bay leaf
parsley sprig
salt and pepper

1 Melt the butter in a large heavy-based saucepan, then cook the bacon, onion and carrot, stirring occasionally, until the vegetables are soft and beginning to colour.

2 Add the celery to the saucepan and cook over a medium heat for 2–3 minutes, stirring occasionally.

3 Stir in the stock, bay leaf, parsley and seasoning and bring to the boil. Cover and simmer gently for about 25 minutes, until the celery is tender and there is almost no liquid left. Serve hot.

> **COOK'S TIP**
> If you are cooking this dish for vegetarians, you can omit the bacon and scatter over some chopped toasted almonds instead.

CAULIFLOWER WITH THREE CHEESES

The flavour of three cheeses gives a new twist to cauliflower cheese.

INGREDIENTS

Serves 4
4 baby cauliflowers
250ml/8fl oz/1 cup single cream
75g/3oz dolcelatte cheese, diced
75g/3oz mozzarella cheese, diced
45ml/3 tbsp freshly grated Parmesan cheese
freshly grated nutmeg
black pepper
toasted breadcrumbs, to garnish

COOK'S TIP
If little baby cauliflowers are not available, you could use one large cauliflower. Divide into quarters and then remove the central core.

1 Cook the cauliflowers in a large pan of boiling salted water for 8–10 minutes, until just tender.

2 Meanwhile, put the cream into a small pan with the cheeses. Heat gently until the cheeses have melted, stirring occasionally. Season with nutmeg and freshly ground pepper.

3 When the cauliflowers are cooked, drain them thoroughly and place one on each of four warmed plates.

4 Spoon a little of the cheese sauce over each cauliflower and sprinkle each with a few of the toasted breadcrumbs. Serve at once.

WINTER VEGETABLE HOT-POT

Use whatever vegetables you have to hand in this richly flavoured and substantial one-pot meal.

INGREDIENTS

Serves 4
2 onions, sliced
4 carrots, sliced
1 small swede, sliced
2 parsnips, sliced
3 small turnips, sliced
½ celeriac, cut into matchsticks
2 leeks, thinly sliced
1 garlic clove, chopped
1 bay leaf, crumbled
30ml/2 tbsp chopped fresh mixed herbs, such as parsley and thyme
300ml/½ pint/1¼ cups vegetable stock
15ml/1 tbsp plain flour
675g/1½ lb red-skinned potatoes, scrubbed and thinly sliced
50g/2oz/4 tbsp butter
salt and black pepper

1 Preheat the oven to 190°C/375°F/ Gas 5. Arrange all the vegetables, except the potatoes, in layers in a large casserole with a tight-fitting lid.

2 Season the vegetable layers lightly with salt and pepper and sprinkle them with garlic, crumbled bay leaf and chopped herbs as you go.

3 Blend the stock into the flour and pour over the vegetables. Arrange the potatoes in overlapping layers on top. Dot with butter and cover tightly.

4 Cook in the oven for 1¼ hours, or until the vegetables are tender. Remove the lid from the casserole and cook for a further 15–20 minutes until the top layer of potatoes is golden and crisp at the edges. Serve hot.

BRAISED RED CABBAGE

Lightly spiced with a sharp, sweet flavour, braised red cabbage goes well with roast pork, duck and game dishes.

INGREDIENTS

Serves 4–6
1kg/2 lb red cabbage
2 onions, chopped
2 cooking apples, peeled, cored and coarsely grated
5ml/1 tsp freshly grated nutmeg
1.25ml/¼ tsp ground cloves
1.25ml/¼ tsp ground cinnamon
15ml/1 tsp dark brown sugar
45ml/3 tbsp red wine vinegar
25g/1oz/2 tbsp butter or margarine, diced
salt and pepper

1 Preheat the oven to 160°C/325°F/ Gas 3. Cut away and discard the large white ribs from the outer cabbage leaves using a large sharp knife, then finely shred the cabbage.

> COOK'S TIP
> This recipe can be cooked in advance. Bake the cabbage for 1½ hours, then leave to cool. To complete the cooking, bake in the oven at 160°C/325°F/Gas 3 for about 30 minutes, stirring occasionally.

2 Layer the shredded cabbage in a large ovenproof dish with the onions, apples, spices, sugar and seasoning. Pour over the vinegar and add the diced butter or margarine.

3 Cover the ovenproof dish and cook in the oven for about 1½ hours, stirring a couple of times, until the cabbage is very tender. Serve hot.

LEMONY CARROTS

The carrots are cooked until just tender in lemony stock which is then thickened to make a light, tangy sauce.

── **INGREDIENTS** ──

Serves 4
600ml/1 pint/2½ cups water
450g/1 lb carrots, thinly sliced
bouquet garni
15ml/1 tbsp lemon juice
pinch of freshly grated nutmeg
20g/¾oz/1½ tbsp butter
15ml/1 tbsp plain (all-purpose) flour
salt and pepper

1 Bring the water to the boil in a large pan, then add the carrots, bouquet garni, lemon juice, nutmeg and seasoning and simmer until the carrots are tender.

2 Remove the carrots using a slotted spoon, then keep warm.

3 Boil the cooking liquid hard until reduced to 300ml/½ pint/1¼ cups. Discard the bouquet garni.

4 Mash 15g/½oz/1 tbsp butter and the flour together, then gradually whisk into the simmering reduced cooking liquid, whisking well after each addition, then simmer for about 3 minutes, until the sauce has thickened.

5 Return the carrots to the pan, heat through in the sauce, then remove from the heat, stir in the remaining butter and serve immediately.

PARSNIPS WITH ALMONDS

Parsnips have an affinity with most nuts, so you could substitute walnuts or hazelnuts (filberts) for the almonds.

INGREDIENTS

Serves 4
450g/1 lb small parsnips
35g/1¼oz/scant 3 tbsp butter
25g/1oz/¼ cup flaked almonds
15ml/1 tbsp soft light brown sugar
pinch of ground mixed spice
15ml/1 tbsp lemon juice
salt and pepper
chopped fresh chervil or parsley, to garnish

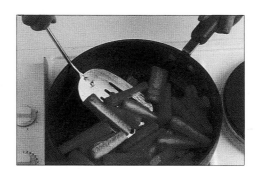

1 Cook the parsnips in boiling salted water until almost tender. Drain well. When the parsnips are cool enough to handle, cut each in half across its width. Quarter the wide halves lengthways.

2 Heat the butter in a frying pan. Add the parsnips and almonds and cook gently, stirring and turning the parsnips carefully until they are lightly flecked with brown.

3 Mix together the sugar and mixed spice, sprinkle over the parsnips and stir to mix, then trickle over the lemon juice. Season and heat for 1 minute. Serve sprinkled with chopped fresh chervil or parsley.

COOK'S TIP
You could replace the ground allspice with Chinese five spice powder, if you prefer.

TURNIPS WITH ORANGE

Sprinkle toasted nuts such as flaked almonds or chopped walnuts or hazelnuts (filberts) over the turnips to add a contrasting texture and taste.

INGREDIENTS

Serves 4
50g/2oz/4 tbsp butter
15ml/1 tbsp oil
1 small shallot, finely chopped
450g/1lb small turnips, quartered
300ml/½ pint/1¼ cups freshly squeezed orange juice
salt and pepper

1 Heat the butter and oil in a saucepan, then cook the shallot gently, stirring occasionally, until soft but not coloured.

2 Add the turnips to the shallot and heat, shaking the pan frequently, until the turnips seem to be absorbing the butter and oil.

3 Pour the orange juice on to the turnips, then simmer gently for about 30 minutes, until the turnips are tender and the orange juice reduced to a buttery sauce.

COOK'S TIP
You could add some spice such as ground ginger, cinnamon or crushed cumin seeds.

CREAMY POTATO GRATIN WITH HERBS

— INGREDIENTS —

Serves 4

675g/1½lb waxy potatoes
25g/1oz/2 tbsp butter
1 onion, finely chopped
1 garlic clove, crushed
2 eggs
300ml/½ pint/1¼ cups crème fraîche or
  double cream
115g/4oz Gruyère cheese, grated
60ml/4 tbsp chopped fresh mixed
  herbs, such as chervil, thyme, chives
  and parsley
freshly grated nutmeg
salt and black pepper

1 Place a baking sheet in the oven and preheat to 190°C/375°F/ Gas 5.

2 Peel the potatoes and cut into matchsticks. Set aside. Melt the butter in a pan and fry the onion and garlic until softened. In a large bowl whisk together the eggs, crème fraîche or cream and half of the cheese.

3 Stir in the onion mixture, herbs, potatoes, salt, pepper and nutmeg. Spoon into a buttered ovenproof dish and sprinkle over the remaining cheese. Bake on the hot baking sheet for 50–60 minutes, until golden brown.

SPINACH ROULADE WITH MUSHROOMS

— INGREDIENTS —

Serves 6–8

450g/1lb fresh spinach
15g/½oz/1 tbsp butter
4 eggs, separated
freshly grated nutmeg
50g/2oz Cheddar cheese, grated
salt and black pepper

For the filling

25g/1oz/2 tbsp butter
350g/12oz button mushrooms,
  chopped
25g/1oz/¼ cup plain flour
150ml/¼ pint/⅔ cup milk
45ml/3 tbsp double cream
30ml/2 tbsp snipped fresh chives

1 Preheat the oven to 190°C/375°F/ Gas 5. Line a 23 x 33cm/9 x 13in Swiss roll tin with non-stick baking paper. Wash the spinach and remove the stalks, then cook the wet leaves in a covered pan without extra water until just tender. Drain the spinach well, squeeze out all the excess moisture and then chop finely.

2 Tip the spinach into a bowl, beat in the butter and egg yolks and season with salt, pepper and nutmeg. Whisk the egg whites until stiff and fold into the spinach mixture. Spread into the tin and sprinkle with half the cheese. Bake for 10–12 minutes, until just firm.

3 Meanwhile, make the filling. Melt the butter in a pan and fry the mushrooms until tender, stir in the flour and cook for 1 minute. Gradually add the milk, then bring to the boil, stirring until thickened. Simmer for a further 2–3 minutes. Remove from the heat and stir in the cream and chives.

4 Remove the cooked roulade from the oven and turn out on to a sheet of non-stick baking paper. Peel off the lining paper and spread the roulade evenly with the mushroom filling.

5 Roll up the roulade fairly tightly and transfer to an ovenproof dish. Sprinkle over the remaining cheese and return the roulade to the oven for about 4–5 minutes to melt the cheese. Serve at once, cut into slices.

CABBAGE WITH BACON

Bacon, especially if smoked, makes all the difference to the flavour of cabbage, turning it into a delicious vegetable accompaniment to serve with roast beef, chicken or even the Christmas turkey.

──── INGREDIENTS ────

30ml/2 tbsp oil
1 onion, finely chopped
115g/4oz smoked bacon, finely chopped
500g/1¼ lb cabbage, shredded
salt and pepper

1 Heat the oil in a large saucepan, add the onion and bacon and cook for about 7 minutes, stirring occasionally.

2 Add the cabbage and salt and pepper. Stir for a few minutes over a medium-high heat until the cabbage begins to lose volume.

3 Continue to cook the cabbage, stirring it frequently, for 8–10 minutes until tender, but still crisp. (For softer cabbage, cover the pan for part of the cooking.)

COOK'S TIP
This dish is equally delicious if you use spring greens (spring cabbage) instead of cabbage. To make a more substantial dish to serve for lunch or supper, add some chopped button mushrooms and skinned, seeded and chopped tomatoes.

LETTUCE AND HERB SALAD

Shops now sell many different types of lettuce leaves all year, so try to use a mixture. Look out for pre-packed bags of mixed baby lettuce leaves.

──── INGREDIENTS ────

Serves 4
½ cucumber
mixed lettuce leaves
1 bunch watercress, about 115g/4oz
1 chicory head, sliced
45ml/3 tbsp mixed chopped fresh
herbs such as parsley, thyme,
tarragon, chives and chervil

For The Dressing
15ml/1 tbsp white wine vinegar
5ml/1 tsp prepared mustard
75ml/5 tbsp olive oil
salt and pepper

1 To make the dressing, mix the vinegar and mustard together, then whisk in the oil and seasoning.

2 Peel the cucumber, if liked, then halve the cucumber lengthways and scoop out the seeds. Thinly slice the flesh. Tear the lettuce leaves into bite-sized pieces.

3 Either toss the cucumber, lettuce, watercress, chicory and herbs together in a bowl, or arrange them in the bowl in layers.

4 Stir the dressing, then pour over the salad, toss lightly to coat the salad vegetables and leaves. Serve at once.

> **COOK'S TIP**
> Do not dress the salad until just before serving otherwise the lettuce leaves will wilt.

COLESLAW WITH CARAWAY

INGREDIENTS

Serves 8
250ml/8fl oz/1 cup mayonnaise
120ml/4fl oz/½ cup white
  wine vinegar
15ml/1 tbsp Dijon mustard
10ml/2 tsp caster sugar
15ml/1 tbsp caraway seeds
1 white cabbage, finely sliced
2 carrots, grated
1 small onion, finely sliced
salt and black pepper
fresh parsley sprigs, to garnish

1 Mix together the mayonnaise, vinegar, mustard, sugar and caraway seeds. Season well.

2 Place the cabbage, carrots and sliced onions in a large bowl.

3 Add the dressing to the vegetables and mix well. Taste for seasoning, then cover and chill for about 1–2 hours. Stir the coleslaw and serve garnished with parsley sprigs.

FRIED TOMATOES WITH CREAM

INGREDIENTS

Serves 4
225g/8oz large firm red tomatoes
40g/1½oz/3 tbsp plain flour
50g/2oz/4 tbsp butter or bacon dripping
sugar, to taste
4 slices hot buttered toast
175ml/6fl oz/¾ cup single cream
salt and black pepper
fresh parsley sprigs, to garnish

1 Slice the tomatoes into 1cm/½in rounds and coat lightly with flour.

2 Heat the butter or bacon fat in a frying pan. When it is hot, add the tomato slices and cook until browned. Turn them once, and season generously with salt and pepper.

3 If the tomatoes are green, sprinkle each slice with a little sugar. Cook for a further 3–4 minutes, until the other side is well browned.

4 Divide the tomatoes among the slices of toast and keep hot.

5 Pour the cream into the hot frying pan and bring to simmering point. Cook for 1–2 minutes, stirring to mix in the cooking juices. Spoon the sauce over the tomatoes, and serve immediately garnished with parsley.

> **VARIATION**
> To make Fried Tomatoes with Ham, top the toast with ham slices before covering with the tomatoes.

Spinach and Beetroot Salad

Ingredients

Serves 4–6
45ml/3 tbsp light olive oil
5–6.25ml/1–1¼ tsp caraway seeds
juice of 1 orange
5ml/1 tsp caster (superfine) sugar
675g/1½ lb cooked beetroot (beets),
  diced
salt and pepper
young spinach leaves, to serve
chopped fresh parsley, to garnish

1 Arrange the spinach leaves in a shallow salad bowl.

2 Heat the oil in a saucepan, add the caraway seeds, orange juice, sugar and salt and pepper.

3 Add the beetroot (beets) and shake the pan to coat it with the dressing.

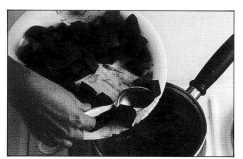

4 Spoon the warm beetroot (beets) and dressing mixture in amongst the spinach and sprinkle with the chopped parsley. Serve at once with roast pork, duck or game.

Cook's Tip
Use freshly cooked beetroot (beets), not those that have been steeped in vinegar.

Beans with Tomatoes

Young runner beans (green beans) should not have 'strings' down the sides, but older ones will and they should be removed before cooking.

Ingredients

Serves 4
675g/1½ lb runner (green) beans, sliced
40g/1½ oz/3 tbsp butter
4 ripe tomatoes, peeled and chopped
salt and pepper
chopped fresh tarragon, to garnish

Cook's Tip
French beans can be used instead of runner (green) beans, but reduce the cooking time slightly.

1 Add the beans to a saucepan of boiling water, return to the boil, then boil for 3 minutes. Drain well.

2 Heat the butter in a saucepan and add the tomatoes, beans and seasoning. Cover the pan and simmer gently for 10–15 minutes, until the beans are tender.

3 Tip the beans and tomatoes into a warm serving dish and sprinkle over the chopped tarragon. Serve hot as an accompaniment to grilled meats, poultry or fish.

WARM CHICKEN LIVER SALAD

Although warm salads may seem over-fussy or trendy, there are times when they are just right. Serve this delicious combination as either a starter or a light meal, with hunks of bread to dip into the dressing.

INGREDIENTS

Serves 4

115g/4oz each fresh young spinach
leaves, rocket and lollo rosso lettuce
2 pink grapefruit
90ml/6 tbsp sunflower oil
10ml/2 tsp sesame oil
10ml/2 tsp soy sauce
225g/8oz chicken livers, chopped
salt and black pepper

1 Wash, dry and tear up all the leaves. Mix them together well in a large salad bowl.

2 Carefully cut away all the peel and white pith from the grapefruit, then neatly segment them catching all the juices in a bowl. Add the grapefruit segments to the leaves in the bowl.

3 To make the dressing, mix together 60ml/4 tbsp of the sunflower oil with the sesame oil, soy sauce, seasoning and grapefruit juice to taste.

4 Heat the rest of the sunflower oil in a small pan and cook the liver, stirring gently, until firm and lightly browned.

5 Tip the chicken livers and dressing over the salad and serve at once.

NEW POTATO AND CHIVE SALAD

The secret of a good potato salad is to mix the potatoes with the dressing while they are still hot so that they absorb it.

─────── INGREDIENTS ───────

Serves 4–6

675g/1½ lb new potatoes (unpeeled)
4 spring onions (scallions)
45ml/3 tbsp olive oil
15ml/1 tbsp white wine vinegar
3.75ml/¾ tsp Dijon mustard
175ml/6 fl oz/¾ cup mayonnaise
45ml/3 tbsp chopped fresh chives
salt and pepper

1 Cook the potatoes in boiling salted water until tender. Meanwhile, finely chop the white parts of the spring onions (scallions) along with a little of the green part.

2 Whisk together the oil, vinegar and mustard. Drain the potatoes well, then immediately toss lightly with the vinegar mixture and spring onions (scallions) and leave to cool.

3 Stir the mayonnaise and chives into the potatoes and chill well until ready to serve with grilled pork, lamb chops or roast chicken.

COOK'S TIP
Look out for the small, waxy potatoes, sold especially for salads and cold dishes – they are particularly good in this recipe.

HOT PUDDINGS

Hot puddings originally meant a range of savoury dishes; the term did not allude to sweet dishes until the beginning of the eighteenth century. Initially the puddings were put on the table alongside savoury dishes, and it was not for a further century or so that sweet puddings were served as they are today – as a separate course, after the main savoury dishes. In this role they became such an institution that names like Queen of Puddings and Cabinet Pudding can evoke keen nostalgia in people who remember them from nursery and childhood days. Comforting Bread and Butter Pudding and Baked Rice Pudding prompt similar reactions, while dishes such as Kentish Cherry Batter Pudding and a wealth of apple recipes are reminders of seasonal fruit harvests.

QUEEN OF PUDDINGS

This pudding was developed from a seventeenth century recipe by Queen Victoria's chefs at Buckingham Palace and named in honour of the monarch.

INGREDIENTS

Serves 4

75g/3oz/1½ cups fresh breadcrumbs
60ml/4 tbsp caster (superfine) sugar,
  plus 5ml/1 tsp
grated rind of 1 lemon
600ml/1 pint/2½ cups milk
4 eggs
45ml/3 tbsp raspberry jam, warmed

1 Stir the breadcrumbs, 30ml/2 tbsp of the sugar and the lemon rind together in a bowl. Bring the milk to the boil in a saucepan, then stir into the breadcrumbs.

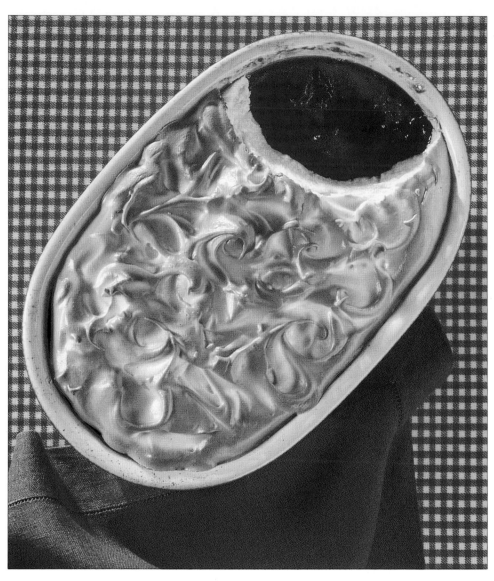

2 Separate three of the eggs and beat the yolks with the whole egg. Stir into the breadcrumb mixture, pour into a buttered baking dish and leave to stand for 30 minutes.

3 Meanwhile, preheat the oven to 160°C/325°F/Gas 3. Bake the pudding for 50–60 minutes, until set.

> **COOK'S TIP**
> The traditional recipe calls for raspberry jam, but you may like to ring the changes by replacing it with another flavoured jam, lemon curd, marmalade or fruit purée.

4 Whisk the egg whites in a large, clean bowl until stiff but not dry, then gradually whisk in the remaining 30ml/2 tbsp caster (superfine) sugar until the mixture is thick and glossy, taking care not to overwhip.

5 Spread the jam over the pudding, then spoon over the meringue to cover the top completely. Sprinkle the remaining sugar over the meringue, then bake for a further 15 minutes, until the meringue is beginning to turn a light golden colour.

PEAR AND BLACKBERRY BROWN BETTY

All this delicious fruity pudding needs to go with it is some hot, home-made custard, pouring cream or ice cream.

INGREDIENTS

Serves 4–6
75g/3oz/6 tbsp butter, diced
175g/6oz/3 cups breadcrumbs made from 1-day-old bread
450g/1 lb ripe pears
450g/1 lb blackberries
grated rind and juice of 1 small orange
115g/4oz/scant ½ cup demerara sugar
demerara sugar, for sprinkling

1 Preheat the oven to 180°C/350°F/ Gas 4. Heat the butter in a heavy frying pan over a moderate heat, add the breadcrumbs and stir until golden.

2 Peel and core the pears, then cut them into thick slices and mix with the blackberries, orange rind and juice.

3 Mix the demerara sugar with the breadcrumbs, then layer with the fruit in a 900ml/1½ pint/3 cup buttered baking dish, beginning and ending with a layer of sugared breadcrumbs.

4 Sprinkle the extra demerara sugar over the top. Cover the baking dish, then bake the pudding for 20 minutes. Uncover the pudding, then bake for a further 30–35 minutes, until the fruit is cooked and the top brown and crisp.

VARIATION
To make Apple and Raspberry Brown Betty, substitute tart eating apples for the pears and use fresh, but not too ripe, raspberries in place of the blackberries.

STICKY TOFFEE PUDDING

INGREDIENTS

Serves 6

*115g/4oz/1 cup toasted walnuts,
 chopped*
175g/6oz/¾ cup butter
175g/6oz/scant 1 cup soft brown sugar
60ml/4 tbsp double (heavy) cream
30ml/2 tbsp lemon juice
2 eggs, beaten
*115g/4oz/1 cup self-raising (self-
 rising) flour*

1 Grease a 900ml/1½ pint/¾ cup pudding basin and add half the nuts.

2 Heat 50g/2oz/4 tbsp of the butter with 50g/2oz/4 tbsp of the sugar, the cream and 15ml/1 tbsp lemon juice in a small pan, stirring until smooth. Pour half into the pudding basin, then swirl to coat it a little way up the sides.

3 Beat the remaining butter and sugar until light and fluffy, then gradually beat in the eggs. Fold in the flour and the remaining nuts and lemon juice and spoon into the basin.

4 Cover the basin with greaseproof (wax) paper with a pleat folded in the centre, then tie securely with string.

5 Steam the pudding for about 1¼ hours, until set in the centre.

6 Just before serving, gently warm the remaining sauce. Unmould the pudding on to a warm plate and pour over the warm sauce.

EASY CHOCOLATE AND ORANGE SOUFFLES

The base in this soufflé is an easy-to-make semolina mixture, rather than the thick white sauce that most soufflés call for.

INGREDIENTS

Serves 4

50g/2oz/generous ⅓ cup semolina
50g/2oz/scant ¼ cup soft brown sugar
600ml/1 pint/2½ cups milk
grated rind of 1 orange
90ml/6 tbsp fresh orange juice
3 eggs, separated
*65g/2½ oz plain (semi-sweet)
 chocolate, grated*
icing (confectioner's) sugar, for sprinkling

1 Preheat the oven to 200°C/400°F/ Gas 6. Butter a shallow 1.75 litre/ 3 pint/7½ cup ovenproof dish.

2 Pour the milk into a heavy-based saucepan, sprinkle over the semolina and brown sugar, then heat, stirring the mixture all the time, until boiling and thickened.

3 Remove the pan from the heat; beat in the orange rind and juice, egg yolks and all but 15ml/1 tbsp of the grated chocolate.

4 Whisk the egg whites until stiff but not dry, then lightly fold into the semolina mixture in three batches. Spoon the mixture into the dish and bake for about 30 minutes until just set in the centre and risen. Sprinkle the top with the reserved chocolate and the icing (confectioner's) sugar, then serve immediately.

BAKED STUFFED APPLES

INGREDIENTS

Serves 4

75g/3oz/scant 1 cup ground almonds
25g/1oz/2 tbsp butter, softened
5ml/1 tsp clear honey
1 egg yolk
50g/2oz/⅓ cup dried apricots, chopped
4 cooking apples, preferably Bramleys

1 Preheat the oven to 200°C/400°F/ Gas 6. Beat together the almonds, butter, honey, egg yolk and apricots.

2 Stamp out the cores from the cooking apples using a large apple corer, then score a line with the point of a sharp knife around the circumference of each apple.

3 Lightly grease a shallow baking dish, then arrange the cooking apples in the dish.

4 Divide the apricot mixture among the cavities in the apples, then bake for 45–60 minutes, until the apples are fluffy.

> **COOK'S TIP**
> If cooking apples are unavailable, use four large, tart eating apples.

KENTISH CHERRY BATTER PUDDING

Kent, known as the 'Garden of England', has been particularly well-known for cherries and the dishes made from them.

INGREDIENTS

Serves 4

45ml/3 tbsp kirsch (optional)
450g/1lb dark cherries, pitted
50g/2oz/½ cup plain (all-purpose) flour
50g/2oz/4 tbsp caster (superfine) sugar
2 eggs, separated
300ml/½ pint/¼ cups milk
75g/3oz/5 tbsp butter, melted
caster (superfine) sugar, for sprinkling

1 Sprinkle the kirsch, if using, over the cherries in a small bowl and leave them to soak for about 30 minutes.

2 Mix the flour and sugar together, then slowly stir in the egg yolks and milk to make a smooth batter. Stir in half the butter and leave for 30 minutes.

3 Preheat the oven to 220°C/425°F/ Gas 7. Pour the remaining butter into a 600 ml/1 pint/2½ cup baking dish and put in the oven to heat.

4 Whisk the egg whites until stiff, then fold into the batter with the cherries and kirsch, if using. Pour into the dish and bake for 15 minutes.

5 Reduce the oven temperature to 180°C/350°F/Gas 4 and bake for 20 minutes, or until golden and set in the centre. Serve sprinkled with sugar.

CIDER PIE

—— INGREDIENTS ——

Serves 6
175g/6oz/1½ cups plain flour
1.25ml/¼ tsp salt
10ml/2 tsp sugar
115g/4oz/½ cup cold butter or
   margarine
50ml/2fl oz/¼ cup or more iced water

For the filling
15g/½oz/1 tbsp butter
250ml/8fl oz/1 cup maple syrup
50ml/2fl oz/¼ cup water
600ml/1 pint/2½ cups cider
2 eggs, at room temperature,
   separated
5ml/1 tsp grated nutmeg

3 Meanwhile, place the cider in a saucepan and boil until only 175ml/6fl oz/¾ cup remains, then cool.

4 Roll out the pastry between two sheets of greaseproof or non-stick baking paper to 3mm/⅛in thickness. Use to line a 23cm/9in pie dish.

5 Trim around the edge, leaving a 1cm/½in overhang. Fold the overhang under to form the edge. Using a fork, press the edge to the rim of the dish and press up from under with your fingers at intervals to make a ruffle effect. Chill the pastry case for at least 20 minutes. Preheat the oven to 180°C/350°F/Gas 4.

6 To make the filling, place the butter, maple syrup, water and cider in a pan and simmer gently for 5–6 minutes. Remove the pan from the heat and leave the mixture to cool slightly, then whisk in the beaten egg yolks.

7 Whisk the egg whites in a large bowl, until they form stiff peaks. Add the cider mixture and fold gently together until evenly blended.

8 Pour the mixture into the prepared pastry case. Dust with the grated nutmeg. Bake the pie for 30–35 minutes, until the pastry is golden brown and the filling is well set and golden. Serve warm.

1 To make the pastry, sift the flour, salt and sugar into a bowl. Using a pastry blender or two knives, cut the butter or margarine into the dry ingredients as quickly as possible until the mixture resembles breadcrumbs.

2 Sprinkle the iced water over the flour mixture. Combine with a fork until the dough holds together. If the dough is too crumbly, add a little more water, 15ml/1 tbsp at a time. Gather the dough into a ball and flatten into a round. Place in a sealed polythene bag and chill for at least 20 minutes.

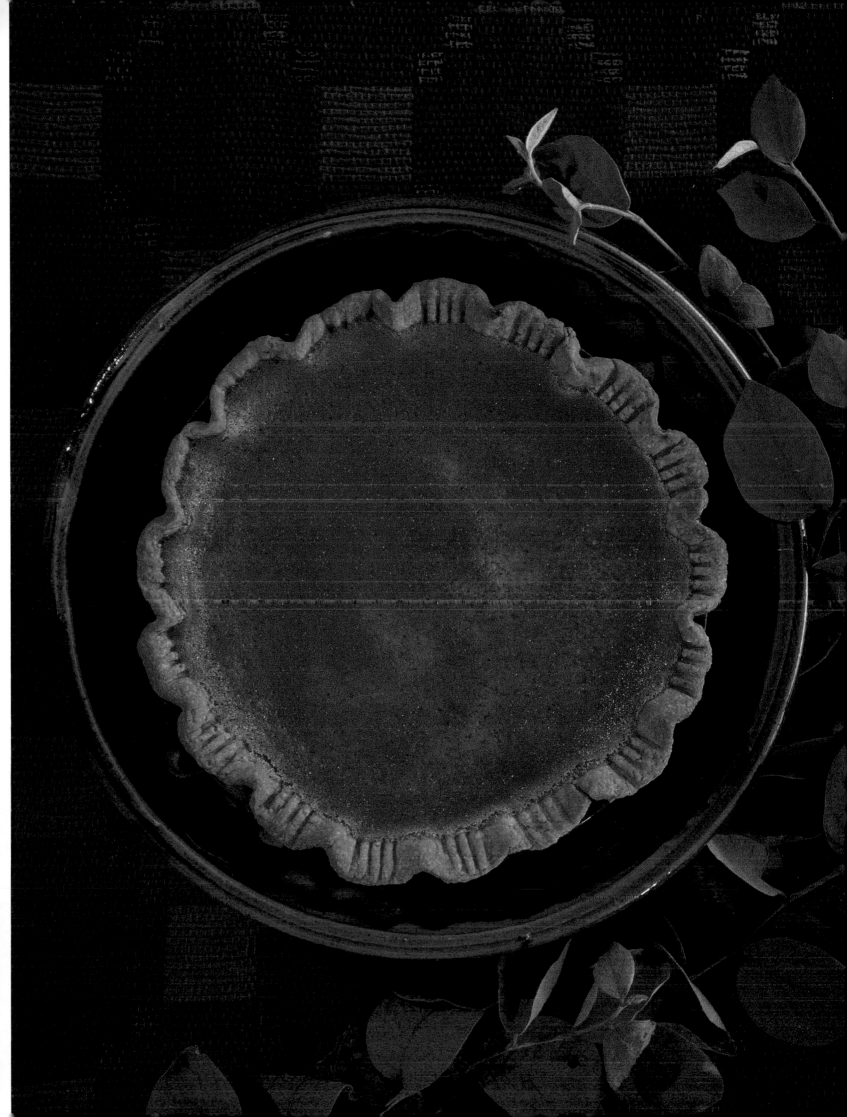

LEMON AND ORANGE WHOLEMEAL TART

INGREDIENTS

Serves 8–10

115g/4oz/1 cup plain flour, sifted
115g/4oz/1 cup plain wholemeal flour
25g/1oz/2 tbsp ground hazelnuts
25g/1oz/3 tbsp icing sugar, sifted
pinch of salt
115g/4oz/½ cup unsalted butter
60ml/4 tbsp lemon curd
300ml/½ pint/1¼ cups whipped cream
   or fromage frais
4 oranges, peeled and thinly sliced

1 Place the flours, hazelnuts, sugar, salt and butter in a food processor and process in short bursts until the mixture resembles breadcrumbs. Add 30–45ml/2–3 tbsp cold water and process until the dough comes together.

2 Turn out on to a lightly floured surface and knead gently until smooth. Roll out and line a 25cm/10in flan tin. Be sure not to stretch the pastry and gently ease it into the corners. Chill for 20 minutes. Preheat the oven to 190°C/375°F/Gas 5.

3 Line the pastry with greaseproof paper and fill with baking beans or bread crusts. Bake 'blind' for 15 minutes, remove the paper and continue for a further 5–10 minutes, until the pastry is crisp. Allow to cool.

4 Whisk the lemon curd into the cream or fromage frais and spread over the base of the pastry. Arrange the orange slices on top and serve at room temperature.

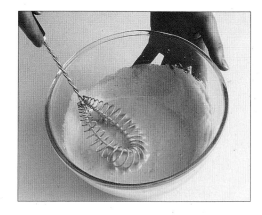

RHUBARB MERINGUE PIE

Serves 6

200g / 7oz / 1¾ cups plain flour
25g / 1oz / ⅓ cup ground walnuts
115g / 4oz / ½ cup butter, diced
275g / 10oz / generous 1½ cups
 caster sugar
4 egg yolks
675g / 1½lb rhubarb, cut into
 small pieces
finely grated rind and juice of 3
 blood or navel oranges
75ml / 5 tbsp cornflour
3 egg whites
whipped cream, to serve

1 Sift the flour into a bowl and add the ground walnuts. Rub in the butter until the mixture resembles fine breadcrumbs. Stir in 30ml/2 tbsp of the sugar with 1 egg yolk beaten with 15ml/1 tbsp water. Mix to a firm dough. Turn out on to a floured surface and knead lightly. Wrap in a polythene bag and chill for at least 30 minutes.

2 Preheat the oven to 190°C/375°F/ Gas 5. Roll out the pastry on a lightly floured surface and use to line a 23cm/9in fluted flan tin. Prick the base with a fork. Line with greaseproof paper and fill with baking beans, then bake for 15 minutes.

3 Meanwhile, put the rhubarb, 75g/3oz/6 tbsp of the remaining sugar and the orange rind in a pan. Cover and cook over a low heat until the rhubarb is tender.

4 Remove the beans and paper, then brush all over with a little of the remaining egg yolks. Bake for a further 10–15 minutes, until the pastry is crisp.

5 Blend the cornflour with the orange juice. Off the heat, stir the cornflour mixture into the rhubarb, then bring to the boil, stirring constantly until thickened. Cook for 1–2 minutes. Cool slightly, then beat in the remaining egg yolks. Pour into the flan case.

6 Whisk the egg whites until they form soft peaks, then whisk in the remaining sugar, 15ml/1 tbsp at a time, whisking well after each addition.

7 Swirl the meringue over the filling to cover completely. Bake for about 25 minutes until golden, then leave to cool for about 30 minutes before serving with whipped cream.

PLUM AND WALNUT CRUMBLE

Walnuts add a lovely crunch to the fruit layer in this crumble – almonds would be equally good.

INGREDIENTS

Serves 4–6

75g/3oz/¾ cup walnut pieces
75g/3oz/6 tbsp butter or hard
  margarine, diced
175g/6oz/1½ cups plain (all-purpose)
  flour
175g/6oz/scant 1 cup demerara sugar
1kg/2lb plums, halved and stoned
  (pitted)

1 Preheat the oven to 180°C/350°F/ Gas 4. Spread the nuts on a baking (cookie) sheet and place in the oven for 8–10 minutes, until evenly coloured.

2 Butter a 1.2 litre/2 pint/5 cup baking dish. Put the plums into the dish and stir in the nuts and half of the demerara sugar.

3 Rub the butter or margarine into the flour until the mixture resembles coarse crumbs. Stir in the remaining sugar and continue to rub in until fine crumbs are formed.

4 Cover the fruit with the crumb mixture and press it down lightly. Bake the pudding for about 45 minutes, until the top is golden brown and the fruit tender.

VARIATION
To make Oat and Cinnamon Crumble, substitute rolled oats for half the flour in the crumble mixture and add 2.5–5ml/½–1 tsp ground cinnamon.

BAKED RICE PUDDING

Rice pudding from a can may be convenient, but it does not compare to the tender, creamy home-made version, especially if you like the skin on top.

INGREDIENTS

Serves 4

50g/2oz/¼ cup pudding rice
30ml/2 tbsp soft light brown sugar
50g/2oz/4 tbsp butter
900ml/1½ pints/3¾ cups milk
small strip of lemon rind
freshly grated nutmeg

1 Preheat the oven to 150°C/300°F/ Gas 2. Butter a 1.2 litre/2 pint/5 cup shallow baking dish.

2 Put the rice, sugar and butter into the dish, stir in the milk and lemon rind and sprinkle a little nutmeg over the surface.

3 Bake the rice pudding in the oven for about 2½ hours, stirring after 30 minutes and another couple of times during the next 2 hours until the rice is tender and the pudding has a thick and creamy consistency.

4 If you like skin on top, leave the rice pudding undisturbed for the final 30 minutes cooking (otherwise, stir it again). Serve hot.

VARIATION
Baked rice pudding is even more delicious with fruit, either cooked in it – in which case you might add sultanas (white raisins), raisins or ready-to-eat dried apricots – or, to serve along side, choose sliced fresh peaches or nectarines, raspberries, strawberries or soaked, then lightly poached, prunes.

CABINET PUDDING

INGREDIENTS

Serves 4

25g/1oz/2½ tbsp raisins, chopped
30ml/2 tbsp brandy (optional)
25g/1oz/2½ tbsp glacé (candied)
   cherries, halved
25g/1oz/2 ½ tbsp angelica, chopped
2 trifle sponge cakes, diced
50g/2oz ratafias, crushed
2 eggs
2 egg yolks
30ml/2 tbsp sugar
450ml/¾ pint/1⅞ cups single (light)
   cream or milk
few drops of vanilla essence (extract)

> **COOK'S TIP**
> The pudding can be cooked in an
> ordinary baking dish, if preferred,
> and served from the dish.

1 Soak the raisins in the brandy, if using, for several hours.

2 Butter a 750ml/1¼ pint/3⅔ cup charlotte mould and arrange some of the cherries and angelica in the base.

3 Mix the remaining cherries and angelica with the sponge cakes, ratafias and raisins and brandy, if using and spoon into the mould.

4 Lightly whisk together the eggs, egg yolks and sugar. Bring the cream or milk just to the boil, then stir into the egg mixture with the vanilla essence.

5 Strain the egg mixture into the mould, then leave for 15–30 minutes.

6 Preheat the oven to 160°C/325°F/ Gas 3. Place the mould in a roasting tin (pan), cover with baking paper and pour in boiling water Bake for 1 hour, or until set. Leave for 2–3 minutes, then turn out on to a warm plate.

EVE'S PUDDING

The tempting apples beneath the sponge topping are the reason for the pudding's name.

INGREDIENTS

Serves 4–6

115g/4oz/½ cup butter
115g/4oz/½ cup caster (superfine) sugar
2 eggs, beaten
grated rind and juice of 1 lemon
90g/3½oz/scant 1cup self-raising
   (self-rising) flour
40g/1½ oz/⅓ cup ground almonds
11g/4oz/scant ½ cup soft brown sugar
500–675g 1½ lb cooking apples, cored
   and thinly sliced
25g/1oz/¼ cup flaked almonds

1 Beat together the butter and caster (superfine) sugar in a large mixing bowl until the mixture is very light and fluffy.

2 Gradually beat the eggs into the butter mixture, beating well after each addition, then fold in the lemon rind, flour and ground almonds.

3 Mix the brown sugar, apples and lemon juice, tip into the dish, add the sponge mixture, then the almonds. Bake for 40–45 minutes, until golden.

BLACKBERRY COBBLER

Serves 8

750g/1¾lb blackberries
200g/7oz/1 cup caster sugar, plus 25g/
*   1oz/2 tbsp caster sugar mixed with*
*   1.25ml/¼ tsp grated nutmeg*
25g/1oz/3 tbsp plain flour
grated rind of 1 lemon

For the topping

225g/8oz/2 cups plain flour
200g/7oz/1 cup caster sugar
15ml/1 tbsp baking powder
pinch of salt
250ml/8fl oz/1 cup milk
115g/4oz/½ cup butter, melted

1 Preheat the oven to 180°C/350°F/ Gas 4. Place the blackberries, caster sugar, flour and lemon rind in a large mixing bowl. Stir gently to coat the blackberries, then transfer to a 1.75 litre/3 pint/7½ cup baking dish.

2 To make the topping, sift the flour, sugar, baking powder and salt into a large bowl and set aside. Blend the milk and butter in a large jug.

3 Gradually pour the milk mixture into the dry ingredients and stir until the mixture is just smooth.

4 Spoon the mixture over the blackberries, spreading evenly.

5 Sprinkle the surface with the sugar and nutmeg mixture. Bake for about 50 minutes, until the topping is set and lightly browned. Serve hot.

APPLE SOUFFLÉ OMELETTE

Apples sautéed until they are slightly caramelized make a delicious autumn filling – you could use fresh raspberries or strawberries in the summer.

―――――――― INGREDIENTS ――――――――

Serves 2
4 eggs, separated
30ml/2 tbsp single cream
15ml/1 tbsp caster sugar
15g/½oz/1 tbsp butter
icing sugar, for dredging

For the filling
1 eating apple, peeled, cored and sliced
25g/1oz/2 tbsp butter
30ml/2 tbsp soft light brown sugar
45ml/3 tbsp single cream

1 To make the filling, sauté the apple slices in the butter and sugar until just tender. Stir in the cream and keep warm, while making the omelette.

2 Place the egg yolks in a bowl with the cream and sugar and beat well. Whisk the egg whites until stiff, then fold into the yolk mixture.

3 Melt the butter in a large heavy-based frying pan, pour in the soufflé mixture and spread evenly. Cook for 1 minute until golden underneath, then place under a hot grill to brown the top.

4 Slide the omelette on to a plate, add the apple mixture, then fold over. Sift the icing sugar over thickly, then mark in a criss-cross pattern with a hot metal skewer. Serve immediately.

BREAD AND BUTTER PUDDING

Vary the dried fruit in this pudding according to your preference. Use currants, sultanas, chopped dried apricots or a mixture of several sorts.

INGREDIENTS

Serves 4–6
75g/3oz/6 tbsp butter
6 slices bread, crusts removed
50g/2oz/about ⅓ cup dried fruit
15ml/1 tbsp chopped mixed (candied) peel
50g/2oz/¼ cup soft light brown sugar
3 eggs, beaten
600ml/1 pint/2½ cups milk

1 Butter a 1.2 litre/2 pint/5 cup baking dish. Butter the bread, then cut off the crusts and cut the slices into triangles, squares or fingers.

2 Arrange half of the bread in the baking dish. Scatter over the dried fruit, mixed peel and half the sugar, then add the remaining bread.

3 Beat the eggs and milk together, then pour into the dish. Sprinkle with the remaining sugar and leave for at least 30 minutes. Meanwhile, preheat the oven to 160°C/325°F/ Gas 3. Bake the pudding for 35–40 minutes until set, and the top is crisp.

> **COOK'S TIP**
> For a special occasion, use cream in place of some, or all, of the milk.

APPLE AND ORANGE PIE

INGREDIENTS

Serves 4
400g/14oz ready-made shortcrust (pie) pastry
3 oranges, peeled
1kg/2 lb cooking apples, cored and thickly sliced
30ml/2 tbsp demerara sugar
beaten egg, to glaze
caster (superfine) sugar, for sprinkling

1 Roll out the pastry on a lightly floured surface to 2cm/¾ in larger than the top of a 1.2 litre/2 pint/5 cup pie dish. Cut off a narrow strip around the edge of the pastry and fit on the rim of the pie dish.

> **COOK'S TIP**
> Use any excess pastry to make leaves to decorate the pie.

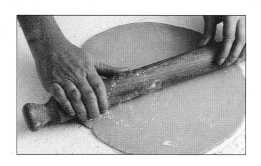

2 Preheat the oven to 190°C/375°F/ Gas 5. Hold one orange at a time over a bowl to catch the juice, cut down between the membranes to remove the segments.

3 Mix the segments and juice, the apples and sugar in the pie dish. Place a pie funnel in the centre of the dish.

4 Dampen the pastry strip. Cover the dish with the rolled out pastry and press the edges to the pastry strip. Brush the top with beaten egg, then bake for 35–40 minutes, until lightly browned. Sprinkle with caster (superfine) sugar before serving.

SURPRISE LEMON PUDDING

The surprise is a delicious, tangy lemon sauce that forms beneath the light topping.

INGREDIENTS

Serves 4
75g/3oz/6 tbsp butter
175g/6oz/⅔ cup soft brown sugar
4 eggs, separated
grated rind and juice of 4 lemons
50g/2oz/½ cup self-raising (self-rising)
  flour
120ml/4 fl oz/½ cup milk

1 Preheat the oven to 180°C/350°F/ Gas mark 4. Butter an 18cm/7 in soufflé dish or cake tin (pan) and stand it in a roasting tin (pan).

2 Beat the butter and sugar together in a large bowl until pale and very fluffy. Beat in 1 egg yolk at a time, beating well after each addition and gradually beating in the lemon rind and juice until well mixed; do not worry if the mixture curdles a little.

3 Sift the flour and stir into the lemon mixture until well mixed, then gradually stir in the milk.

4 Whisk the egg whites in a separate bowl until stiff but not dry, then lightly, but thoroughly, fold into the lemon mixture in three batches. Carefully pour the mixture into the soufflé dish or cake tin (pan), then pour boiling water around.

5 Bake the pudding in the middle of the oven for about 45 minutes, or until risen, just firm to the touch and golden brown on top. Serve at once.

CASTLE PUDDINGS WITH REAL CUSTARD

INGREDIENTS

Serves 4

*about 45ml/3 tbsp blackcurrant,
  strawberry or raspberry jam*
115g/4oz/½ cup butter
*115g/4oz/generous ½ cup caster
  (superfine) sugar*
2 eggs, beaten
few drops of vanilla essence (extract)
*130g/4½oz/generous cup self-raising
  (self-rising) flour*

For The Custard

450ml/¾ pint/scant 1 cup milk
4 eggs
22.5–30ml/1½–2 tbsp sugar
few drops of vanilla essence (extract)

1 Preheat the oven to 180°C/350°F/
Gas 4. Butter eight dariole moulds.
Put about 10ml/2 tsp jam in the base
of each mould.

2 Beat the butter and sugar together
until light and fluffy, then gradually
beat in the eggs, beating well after each
addition and adding the vanilla essence
(extract) towards the end. Lightly fold
in the flour, then divide the mixture
among the moulds.

3 Bake the puddings for about 20
minutes until well risen and a light
golden colour.

4 Meanwhile, make the sauce. Whisk
the eggs and sugar together. Bring
the milk to the boil in a heavy, preferably non-stick, saucepan, then slowly
pour on to the sweetened egg mixture,
stirring constantly.

5 Return the milk to the pan and heat
very gently, stirring, until the mixture thickens enough to coat the back
of a spoon; do not allow to boil. Cover
the pan and remove from the heat.

6 Remove the moulds from the oven,
leave to stand for a few minutes,
then turn the puddings on to warmed
plates and serve with the custard.

COOK'S TIP
Instead of baking the puddings,
you can steam them for 30–40
minutes. If you do not have dariole
moulds, use ramekin dishes.

CHRISTMAS PUDDING

This recipe makes enough to fill one 1.2 litre/2 pint/5 cups basin or two 600ml/1 pint/2½ cups basins. It can be made up to a month before Christmas and stored in a cool, dry place.

INGREDIENTS

Serves 8
115g/4oz/½ cup butter, plus extra
  for greasing
225g/8oz/1 heaped cup soft dark
  brown sugar
50g/2oz/½ cup self-raising flour
5ml/1 tsp mixed spice
1.5ml/¼ tsp grated nutmeg
2.5ml/½ tsp ground cinnamon
2 eggs
115g/4oz/2 cups fresh white
  breadcrumbs
175g/6oz/1 cup sultanas
175g/6oz/1 cup raisins
115g/4oz/½ cup currants
25g/1oz/3 tbsp mixed candied peel,
  chopped finely
25g/1oz/¼ cup chopped almonds
1 small cooking apple, peeled, cored
  and coarsely grated
finely grated rind of 1 orange or lemon
juice of 1 orange or lemon, made up to
  150ml/¼ pint/⅔ cup with brandy, rum
  or sherry

1 Cut a disc of greaseproof paper to fit the base of the basin(s) and butter the disc and basin(s).

2 Whisk the butter and sugar together until soft. Beat in the flour, spices and eggs. Stir in the remaining ingredients thoroughly.

3 Turn the mixture into the basin(s) and level the top. Cover with another disc of buttered greaseproof paper.

4 Make a pleat across the centre of a large piece of greaseproof paper, folding in both directions, and cover the basin(s) with it, tying it in place with string under the rim. Cut off the excess paper.

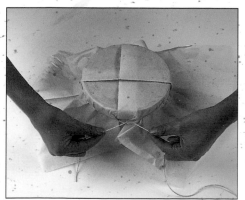

5 Pleat a piece of foil in the same way and cover the basin(s) with it, tucking it around the bowl neatly. Tie another piece of string around the basin(s) and across the top, as a handle.

6 Place the basin(s) in a steamer over a pan of simmering water. Steam for 6 hours if a large pudding, 2 hours for individual puddings. Alternatively, put the basin(s) into a large pan and pour round enough boiling water to come halfway up the basin(s) and cover the pan with a tight-fitting lid. Check the water is simmering and top it up with boiling water as it evaporates. When the pudding(s) have cooked, leave to cool. Remove the foil and greaseproof paper. Wipe the basin(s) clean and replace the greaseproof paper and foil with clean pieces, ready for reheating.

COOK'S TIP
Steam a large pudding for 2 hours before serving; smaller, individual puddings need only 1 hour. Turn on to a plate and leave to stand for 5 minutes, before removing the pudding basin(s). Serve with brandy or rum butter, whisky sauce or custard.

COLD DESSERTS

Britain's agricultural and rural heritage has always provided a plentiful supply of the ingredients needed to make a wide selection of cold desserts. Orchards and hedgerows supplied fruit for fools such as Gooseberry and Elderflower Cream and for Summer Puddings; garden strawberries and raspberries at midsummer were turned into dishes as diverse as Eton Mess, Cranachan and Peach Melba. Jugsful of milk and cream from the dairy were transformed into Honeycomb Mould, junkets such as Damask Cream, syllabubs and blancmanges. Eggs gathered from the hen coop thickened the custard for trifles and enriched the fillings for Yorkshire Curd Tart and Bakewell Tart.

RHUBARB AND GINGER CHEESECAKE

Fresh rhubarb and ginger are natural partners in this quite heavenly cheesecake.

INGREDIENTS

Serves 6

75g/3oz/6 tbsp butter
175g/6oz ginger biscuits, crushed
50g/2oz/½ cup pecan nuts, chopped
350g/12oz rhubarb, chopped
75g/3oz/6 tbsp caster sugar
10ml/2 tsp ginger syrup
3 size 1 eggs, beaten
225g/8oz curd cheese
10ml/2 tsp powdered gelatine
150ml/¼ pint/⅔ cup double cream,
  plus extra whipped cream, to serve

1 Lightly grease a 20cm/8in round loose-bottomed cake tin.

2 Melt the butter in a small pan and stir in the crushed biscuits and pecan nuts. Press the mixture firmly into the base of the tin using a potato masher.

3 Put the rhubarb, sugar and ginger syrup into a pan, cover and cook very gently until soft. Purée in a blender or food processor until smooth.

4 Return the mixture to the pan and beat in the eggs. Cook over a low heat, stirring until the mixture thickens; do not allow it to boil or it will curdle. Remove the pan from the heat and beat in the cheese. Leave to cool.

5 Sprinkle the powdered gelatine over 30ml/2 tbsp cold water and leave to soften for a few minutes. Place the bowl over a pan of simmering water and stir until the gelatine dissolves and the liquid is clear. Cool slightly, then stir into the rhubarb mixture.

6 Whip the cream until it forms soft peaks, then fold into the rhubarb mixture. Pour into the prepared tin and chill until set. Cut into wedges and serve with extra cream.

BLACKBERRY BROWN SUGAR MERINGUE

------- INGREDIENTS -------

Serves 6
175g/6oz/1 cup soft light brown sugar
3 egg whites
5ml/1 tsp distilled malt vinegar
2.5ml/½ tsp vanilla essence

For the filling*
350–450g/12oz–1lb blackberries
30ml/2 tbsp crème de cassis
300ml/½ pint/1¼ cups double cream
15ml/1 tbsp icing sugar, sifted
small blackberry leaves, to decorate
   (optional)

1 Preheat the oven to 160°C/325°F/ Gas 3. Draw a 20cm/8in circle on a sheet of non-stick baking paper, turn over and place on a baking sheet.

2 Spread out the brown sugar on a baking sheet and dry in the oven for 8–10 minutes. Sieve to remove lumps.

3 Whisk the egg whites in a bowl until stiff. Add half the dried brown sugar, 15ml/1 tbsp at a time, whisking well after each addition. Add the vinegar and vanilla essence, then fold in the remaining sugar.

4 Spoon the meringue on to the drawn circle on the paper, leaving a hollow in the centre. Bake for 45 minutes, then turn off the oven and leave the meringue in the oven with the door slightly open, until cold.

5 Place the blackberries in a bowl, sprinkle over the crème de cassis and leave to macerate for 30 minutes.

6 When the meringue is cold, carefully peel off the non-stick baking paper and transfer the meringue to a serving plate. Lightly whip the cream with the icing sugar and spoon into the centre. Top with the blackberries and decorate with small blackberry leaves, if liked. Serve at once.

GOOSEBERRY AND ELDERFLOWER CREAM

When elderflowers are in season, instead of using the cordial, cook two to three elderflower heads with the gooseberries.

INGREDIENTS

Serves 4

500g/1¼ lb gooseberries
300ml/½ pint//1¼ cups double (heavy) cream
about 115g/4 oz/1 cup icing (confectioner's) sugar, to taste
30ml/2 tbsp elderflower cordial or orange flower water (optional)
mint sprigs, to decorate
almond biscuits (cookies), to serve

1 Place the gooseberries in a heavy saucepan, cover and cook over a low heat, shaking the pan occasionally, until the gooseberries are tender. Tip the gooseberries into a bowl, crush them, then leave to cool completely.

2 Beat the cream until soft peaks form, then fold in half the crushed gooseberries. Sweeten and add elder-flower cordial, or orange flower water to taste, if used. Sweeten the remaining gooseberries.

3 Layer the cream mixture and the crushed gooseberries in four dessert dishes or tall glasses, then cover and chill. Decorate with mint sprigs and serve with almond biscuits (cookies).

COOK'S TIP
If preferred, the cooked goose-berries can be puréed and sieved, or try an equivalent quantity of real custard instead of the cream.

ETON MESS

This dish forms part of the picnic meals parents and pupils enjoy on the lawns at Eton College's annual prize-giving in early June.

───── INGREDIENTS ─────

Serves 4

500g/1¼ lb strawberries, chopped
45–60ml/3–4 tbsp kirsch
300ml/½ pint/1¼ cups double (heavy)
    cream
6 small, white meringues
mint sprigs, to decorate

1 Put the strawberries in a bowl, sprinkle over the kirsch, then cover and chill for 2–3 hours.

2 Whip the cream until soft peaks form, then gently fold in the strawberries with their juices.

3 Crush the meringues into rough chunks, then scatter over the strawberry mixture and fold in gently

4 Spoon the strawberry mixture into a glass serving bowl, decorate with mint sprigs and serve immediately.

COOK'S TIP
If you would prefer to make a less rich version, use strained Greek yogurt or thick natural yogurt instead of part or all of the cream. Simply beat the yogurt gently before adding the strawberries.

CRANACHAN

INGREDIENTS

Serves 4

50g/2oz/⅔ cup medium oatmeal
60ml/4 tbsp clear honey
45ml/3 tbsp whisky
300ml/½ pint/1¼ cups double (heavy)
   cream
350g/12oz raspberries
mint sprigs, to decorate

1 Gently warm the honey in the whisky, then leave to cool.

2 Preheat the grill (broiler). Spread the oatmeal in a very shallow layer in the grill (broiler) pan and toast, stirring occasionally, until browned. Leave to cool.

3 Whip the cream in a large bowl until soft peaks form, then gently stir in the oats, honey and whisky until well combined.

4 Reserve a few raspberries for decoration, then layer the remainder with the oat mixture in four tall glasses. Cover and chill for 2 hours.

5 About 30 minutes before serving, transfer the glasses to room temperature. Decorate with the reserved raspberries and mint sprigs.

OLD ENGLISH TRIFLE

INGREDIENTS

Serves 6

75g/3oz day-old sponge cake, broken
   into bite-size pieces
8 ratafias, broken into halves
100ml/3½ fl oz/⅓ cup medium sherry
30ml/2 tbsp brandy
350g/12oz prepared fruit such as
   raspberries, strawberries or peaches
300ml/½ pint/1¼ cups double (heavy)
   cream
40g/1½oz/⅓ cup toasted flaked almonds
strawberies, to decorate

For The Custard

4 egg yolks
25g/1oz/2 tbsp caster (superfine) sugar
450ml/¾ pint/scant 2 cups single
   (light) or whipping cream
few drops of vanilla essence (extract)

1 Put the sponge cake and ratafias in a glass serving dish, then sprinkle over the sherry and brandy and leave until they have been absorbed.

2 To make the custard, whisk the egg yolks and sugar together. Bring the cream to the boil in a heavy saucepan, then pour on to the egg yolk mixture, stirring constantly.

3 Return the mixture to the pan and heat very gently, stirring all the time with a wooden spoon, until the custard thickens enough to coat the back of the spoon; do not allow to boil. Leave to cool, stirring occasionally.

4 Put the fruit in an even layer over the sponge cake in the serving dish, then strain the custard over the fruit and leave to set. Lightly whip the cream, spread it over the custard, then chill the trifle well. Decorate with flaked almonds and strawberries just before serving.

Apple and Mint Hazelnut Shortcake

INGREDIENTS

Serves 8–10

150g/5oz/1 cup plain wholemeal flour
50g/2oz/4 tbsp ground hazelnuts
50g/2oz/4 tbsp icing sugar, sifted
150g/5oz/10 tbsp unsalted butter or
*   margarine*
3 sharp eating apples
5ml/1 tsp lemon juice
15–30ml/1–2 tbsp caster sugar, or to
*   taste*
15ml/1 tbsp chopped fresh mint, or
*   5ml/1 tsp dried*
250ml/8fl oz/1 cup whipping cream or
*   crème fraîche*
few drops vanilla essence
few mint leaves and whole hazelnuts, to
*   decorate*

1 Process the flour, ground hazelnuts and icing sugar with the butter in a food processor in short bursts, or rub the butter into the dry ingredients until they come together. (Don't overwork the mixture.) Bring the dough together, adding a very little iced water if necessary. Knead briefly, wrap in grease-proof paper and chill for 30 minutes.

2 Preheat the oven to 160°C/325°F/ Gas 3. Cut the dough in half and roll out each half, on a lightly floured surface, to an 18cm/7in round. Place on greaseproof paper on baking sheets and bake for about 40 minutes, or until crisp. If browning too much, move them down in the oven to a lower shelf. Allow to cool.

3 Peel, core and chop the apples into a pan with the lemon juice. Add sugar to taste, then cook for 2–3 minutes, until just softening. Mash the apple gently with the chopped fresh mint and leave to cool.

4 Whip the cream with the vanilla essence. Place one shortbread base on a serving plate. Spread half the apple and half the cream or crème fraîche on top .

5 Place the second shortcake on top, then spread over the remaining apple and cream, swirling the top layer of cream gently. Decorate the top with mint leaves and a few whole hazelnuts, then serve at once.

TANGERINE TRIFLE

An unusual variation on a traditional trifle – of course, you can add a little alcohol if you wish.

INGREDIENTS

Serves 4

5 trifle sponges, halved lengthways
30ml/2 tbsp apricot conserve
15–20 ratafia biscuits
142g/4¾ oz packet tangerine jelly
300g/11oz can mandarin oranges,
  drained, reserving juice
600ml/1 pint/2½ cups ready-made (or
  home-made) custard
whipped cream and shreds of orange
  rind, to decorate
caster sugar, for sprinkling

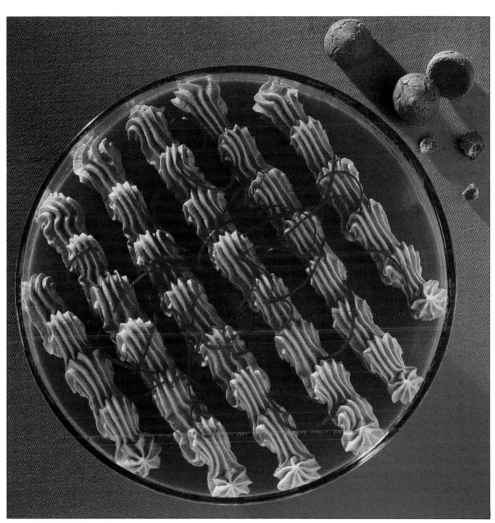

1 Spread the halved sponge cakes with apricot conserve and arrange in the base of a deep serving bowl or glass dish. Sprinkle over the ratafias.

2 Break up the jelly into a heatproof measuring jug, add the juice from the canned mandarins and dissolve in a pan of hot water or in the microwave. Stir until the liquid clears.

3 Make up to 600ml/1 pint/2½ cups with ice cold water, stir well and leave to cool, for up to 30 minutes. Scatter the mandarin oranges over the cake and ratafias.

4 Pour the jelly over the mandarin oranges, cake and ratafias and chill for 1 hour, or more.

5 When the jelly has set, pour the custard over the top and chill again.

6 When ready to serve, pipe the whipped cream over the custard. Wash the orange rind shreds, sprinkle them with caster sugar and use to decorate the trifle.

CHERRY SYLLABUB

This recipe follows the style of the earliest syllabubs from the sixteenth and seventeenth centuries, producing a frothy creamy layer over a liquid one.

INGREDIENTS

Serves 4
225g/8oz ripe dark cherries, stoned (pitted) and chopped
30ml/2 tbsp kirsch
2 egg whites
75g/3oz/generous ½ cup caster (superfine) sugar
30ml/2 tbsp lemon juice
150ml/¼ pint/⅔ cup sweet white wine
300ml/½ pint/1¼ cups double (heavy) cream

1 Divide the chopped cherries among six tall dessert glasses and sprinkle over the kirsch.

2 In a clean bowl, whisk the egg whites until stiff. Gently fold in the sugar, lemon juice and wine.

3 In a separate bowl (but using the same whisk), lightly beat the cream, then fold into the egg white mixture.

4 Spoon the cream mixture over the cherries, then chill overnight.

DAMASK CREAM

It is important not to move this simple, light, yet elegant dessert while it is setting, otherwise it will separate.

INGREDIENTS

Serves 4
600ml/1 pint/2½ cups milk
45ml/3 tbsp caster (superfine) sugar
several drops of triple-strength rosewater
10ml/2 tsp rennet
60ml/4 tbsp double (heavy) cream
sugared rose petals, to decorate (optional)

1 Gently heat the milk and 30ml/2 tbsp of the sugar, stirring, until the sugar has melted and the temperature reaches 36.9°C/98.4°F, or the milk feels neither hot nor cold.

2 Stir rosewater to taste into the milk, then remove the pan from the heat and stir in the rennet.

3 Pour the milk into a serving dish and leave undisturbed for 2–3 hours, until set.

4 Stir the remaining sugar into the cream, then carefully spoon over the junket. Decorate with sugared rose petals, if liked.

CHOCOLATE BLANCMANGE

For a special dinner party, flavour the blancmange with peppermint essence (extract), creme de menthe or orange liqueur, and decorate with whipped cream and white and plain chocolate curls.

— INGREDIENTS —

Serves 4

60ml/4 tbsp cornflour (cornstarch)
600ml/1 pint/2½ cups milk
45ml/3 tbsp sugar
50–115g/2–4 oz plain (semi-sweet) chocolate, chopped
few drops vanilla essence (extract)
chocolate curls, to decorate

1 Rinse a 750ml/1¼ pint/3 cup fluted mould with cold water and leave it upside down to drain. Blend the cornflour (cornstarch) to a smooth paste with a little of the milk.

2 Bring the remaining milk to the boil, preferably in a non-stick saucepan, then pour on to the blended mixture stirring all the time.

3 Pour all the milk back into the saucepan and bring slowly to the boil over a low heat, stirring all the time until the mixture boils and thickens. Remove the pan from the heat, then add the sugar, chopped chocolate and vanilla essence (extract) and stir until the sauce is smooth and the chocolate melted.

4 Pour the chocolate mixture into the mould and leave in a cool place for several hours to set.

5 To unmould the blancmange, place on a large serving plate, then holding the plate and mould firmly together, invert them. Give both plate and mould a gentle but firm shake to loosen the blancmange, then lift off the mould. Scatter the white and plain chocolate curls over the top of the blancmange and serve at once.

COOK'S TIP
If you prefer, set the blancmange in four or six individual moulds.

HONEYCOMB MOULD

Home-made Honeycomb
Moulds have a fresh, clear
lemon flavour. They look attractive when unmoulded, as the
mixture sets in layers.

───── INGREDIENTS ─────

Serves 4
30ml/2 tbsp cold water
15g/½oz/1 envelope gelatine
2 eggs, separated
*75g/3oz/scant ½ cup caster (superfine)
  sugar*
475ml/16 fl oz/2 cups milk
grated rind of 1 small lemon
60ml/4 tbsp lemon juice

1 Chill four individual moulds, or a
1.2 litre/2 pint/5 cup jelly mould.

2 Pour the water into a small bowl,
sprinkle over the gelatine and leave
to soften for 5 minutes. Place the bowl
over a small saucepan of hot water and
stir occasionally until dissolved.

3 Meanwhile, whisk the egg yolks
and sugar together until pale, thick
and fluffy.

4 Bring the milk to the boil in a
heavy, preferably non-stick,
saucepan, then slowly pour on to the
egg yolks, stirring.

5 Return the milk mixture to the pan
then heat gently, stirring, until
thickened; do not allow to boil.
Remove from the heat and stir in the
lemon rind and juice.

6 Stir 2 or 3 spoonsful of the lemon
mixture into the gelatine, then stir
back into the saucepan. In a clean dry
bowl, whisk the egg whites until stiff
but not dry, then gently fold into the
mixture in the pan in three batches.

7 Rinse the moulds or mould with
cold water and drain well, then
pour in the lemon mixture. Leave to
cool, then cover and chill until set and
ready to unmould and serve.

PEACH MELBA

The original dish created for the opera singer Dame Nellie Melba had peaches and ice cream served upon an ice swan.

INGREDIENTS

Serves 4
300g/11oz raspberries
squeeze of lemon juice
icing (confectioner's) sugar, to taste
2 large ripe peaches or 425g/15oz can sliced peaches
8 scoops vanilla ice cream

1 Press the raspberries through a non-metallic sieve (strainer).

2 Add a little lemon juice to the raspberry purée and sweeten to taste with icing (confectioner's) sugar.

3 Dip fresh peaches in boiling water for 4–5 seconds, then slip off the skins, halve along the indented line, then slice; or tip canned peaches into a sieve (strainer) and drain.

4 Place two scoops of ice cream in each individual glass dish, top with peach slices, then pour over the raspberry puree. Serve immediately.

COOK'S TIP
If you'd like to prepare this ahead, scoop the ice cream on to a cold baking sheet and freeze until ready to serve, then transfer the scoops to the dishes.

SUMMER PUDDING

INGREDIENTS

about 8 thin slices day-old white bread, crusts removed
800g/1¾lb mixed summer fruits
about 30ml/2 tbsp sugar

1 Cut a round from one slice of bread to fit in the base of a 1.2 litre/ 2 pint/5 cup pudding basin, then cut strips of bread about 5cm/2 in wide to line the basin, overlapping the strips slightly so there are no gaps.

2 Gently heat the fruit, sugar and 30ml/2 tbsp water in a large heavy saucepan, shaking the pan occasionally, until the juices begin to run.

3 Reserve about 45ml/3 tbsp fruit juice, then spoon the fruit and remaining juice into the basin, taking care not to dislodge the bread.

4 Cut the remaining bread to fit entirely over the fruit. Stand the basin on a plate and cover with a saucer or small plate that will just fit inside the top of the basin. Place a heavy weight on top. Chill the pudding and the reserved fruit juice overnight.

5 Run a knife carefully around the inside of the basin rim, then invert the pudding on to a cold serving plate. Pour over the reserved juice and serve.

Frozen Strawberry Mousse Cake

Children love this cake –
because it is pink and pretty, and
it is just like an ice cream treat.

Ingredients

Serves 4–6
425g/15oz can strawberries in syrup
*15ml/1 tbsp/1 sachet powdered
gelatine*
6 trifle sponge cakes
45ml/3 tbsp strawberry conserve
200ml/7fl oz/⅞ cup crème fraîche
*200ml/7fl oz/⅞ cup whipped cream, to
decorate*

1 Strain the syrup from the strawberries into a large heatproof jug. Sprinkle over the gelatine and stir well. Stand the jug in a pan of hot water and stir until the gelatine has dissolved.

2 Leave to cool, then chill for just under 1 hour, until beginning to set. Meanwhile, cut the sponge cakes in half lengthways and spread the cut surfaces with the strawberry conserve.

3 Slowly whisk the crème fraîche into the strawberry jelly, then whisk in the canned strawberries. Line a deep, 20cm/8in loose-based cake tin with non-stick baking paper.

4 Pour half the strawberry mousse mixture into the tin, arrange the sponge cakes over the surface, and then spoon over the remaining mousse mixture, pushing down any sponge cakes which rise up.

5 Freeze for 1–2 hours until firm. Unmould the cake and carefully remove the lining paper. Transfer to a serving plate. Decorate with whirls of cream and a few strawberry leaves and a fresh strawberry, if you have them.

LEMON SOUFFLÉ WITH BLACKBERRIES

The simple fresh taste of the cold lemon mousse combines well with the rich blackberry sauce, and the colour contrast looks wonderful, too. Blueberries or raspberries make equally delicious alternatives to blackberries.

INGREDIENTS

Serves 6
grated rind of 1 lemon and juice of 2
 lemons
1 sachet/15ml/1 tbsp powdered
 gelatine
5 size 4 eggs, separated
150g/5oz/10 tbsp caster sugar
few drops vanilla essence
400ml/14fl oz/1⅔ cups whipping cream

For the sauce
175g/6oz blackberries (fresh or frozen)
30–45ml/2–3 tbsp caster sugar
few fresh blackberries and blackberry
 leaves, to decorate

1 Place the lemon juice in a small pan and heat through. Sprinkle on the gelatine and leave to dissolve or heat further until clear. Allow to cool.

2 Put the lemon rind, egg yolks, sugar and vanilla into a large bowl and whisk until the mixture is very thick, pale and creamy.

3 Whisk the egg whites until stiff and almost peaky. Whip the cream until stiff and holding its shape.

4 Stir the gelatine mixture into the yolks, then fold in the whipped cream and lastly the egg whites. When lightly but thoroughly blended, turn into a 1.5 litre/2½ pint/6 cup soufflé dish and freeze for 2 hours.

5 To make the sauce, place the blackberries in a pan with the sugar and cook for 4–6 minutes until the juices begin to run and all the sugar has dissolved. Pass through a sieve to remove the seeds, then chill until ready to serve.

6 When the soufflé is almost frozen, but still spoonable, scoop or spoon out on to individual plates and serve with the blackberry sauce.

Boodles Orange Fool

This fool became the speciality of Boodles Club, a gentlemen's club in London's St James's.

Ingredients

Serves 4

4 trifle sponge cakes, cubed
300ml/½ pint/1¼ cups double (heavy)
* cream*
30–60ml/2–4 tbsp caster (superfine)
* sugar*
grated rind and juice of 2 oranges
grated rind and juice of 1 lemon
orange and lemon slices and rind, to
* decorate*

1 Line the bottom and halfway up the sides of a large glass serving bowl or china dish with the cubed trifle sponge cakes.

2 Whip the cream with the sugar until it starts to thicken, then gradually whip in the fruit juices, adding the fruit rinds towards the end.

3 Carefully pour the cream mixture into the bowl or dish, taking care not to dislodge the sponge. Cover and chill for 3–4 hours. Serve decorated with orange and lemon slices and rind.

> **Watchpoint**
> Take care not to overwhip the cream mixture.

Apricot And Orange Jelly

Ingredients

Serves 4

350g/12 oz well-flavoured fresh ripe
* apricots, stoned (pitted)*
50–75g/2–3 oz/about ⅓ cup sugar
about 300ml/½ pint/1¼ cups freshly
* squeezed orange juice*
15ml/1 tbsp gelatine
single (light) cream, to serve
finely chopped candied orange peel, to
* decorate*

1 Heat the apricots, sugar and 120ml/4 fl oz/½ cup orange juice, stirring until the sugar has dissolved. Simmer gently until the apricots are tender.

2 Press the apricot mixture through a nylon sieve (strainer) into a small measuring jug.

3 Pour 45 ml/3 tbsp orange juice into a small heatproof bowl, sprinkle over the gelatine and leave for about 5 minutes, until softened.

4 Place the bowl over a saucepan of hot water and heat until the gelatine has dissolved. Slowly pour into the apricot mixture, stirring all the time. Make up to 600ml/1 pint/2½ cups with orange juice.

5 Pour the apricot mixture into four individual dishes and chill until set. Pour a thin layer of cream over the surface of the jellies before serving, decorated with candied orange peel.

YORKSHIRE CURD TART

The distinguishing characteristic of Yorkshire curd tarts is all-spice, or 'clove pepper' as it was known locally.

INGREDIENTS

Serves 8
115g/4oz/½ cup butter, diced
225g/8oz/2 cups plain (all-purpose) flour
1 egg yolk

For The Filling
large pinch of ground allspice
90g/3½oz/½ cup soft light brown sugar
3 eggs, beaten
grated rind and juice of 1 lemon
40g/1½oz/3 tbsp butter, melted
450g/1 lb curd (medium fat soft) cheese
75g/3oz/scant ½ cup raisins or sultanas (white raisins)

1 Toss the butter in the flour, then rub it in until the mixture resembles breadcrumbs. Stir the egg yolk into the flour mixture with a little water to bind the dough together.

2 Turn the dough on to a lightly floured surface, knead lightly and briefly, then form into a ball. Roll out the pastry thinly and use to line a 20cm/8in fluted loose-bottomed flan tin (quiche pan). Chill for 15 minutes.

3 Preheat the oven to 190°C/375°F/Gas 5. To make the filling, mix the ground allspice with the sugar, then stir in the eggs, lemon rind and juice, butter, curd cheese and raisins or sultanas (white raisins).

4 Pour the filling into the pastry case, then bake for about 40 minutes until the the pastry is cooked and the filling is lightly set and golden brown. Serve still slightly warm, cut into wedges, with cream, if you like.

COOK'S TIP
Although it's not traditional, you could easily substitute mixed spice for the ground allspice – the flavour will be slightly different, but just as good in this tart.

BAKEWELL TART

Although the pastry base makes this a tart, the original recipe calls it a pudding.

INGREDIENTS

Serves 4
225g/8oz ready-made puff pastry
30ml/2 tbsp raspberry or apricot jam
2 eggs
2 egg yolks
115g/4oz/generous ½ cup caster (superfine) sugar
115g/4oz/½ cup butter, melted
50g/2oz/⅔ cup ground almonds
few drops of almond essence (extract)
icing (confectioner's) sugar, for sifting

1 Preheat the oven to 200°C/400°F/ Gas 6. Roll out the pastry on a lightly floured surface and use it to line an 18cm/7 in pie plate or loose-based flan tin (quiche pan). Spread the jam over the bottom of the pastry case.

2 Whisk the eggs, egg yolks and sugar together in a large bowl until thick and pale.

3 Gently stir the butter, ground almonds and almond essence (extract) into the mixture.

4 Pour the mixture into the pastry case and bake for 30 minutes, until the filling is just set and browned. Sift icing (confectioner's) sugar over the top before eating hot, warm or cold.

COOK'S TIP
Since this pastry case isn't baked blind first, place a baking sheet in the oven while it preheats, then place the flan tin (quiche pan) on the hot sheet. This will ensure that the bottom of the pastry case cooks right through.

CHOCOLATE DATE TORTE

A stunning cake that tastes wonderful. Rich and gooey – it's a chocaholic's delight!

─────── INGREDIENTS ───────

Serves 8

200g /7oz /scant 1 cup fromage frais
200g /7oz /scant 1 cup mascarpone
icing sugar, to taste
4 egg whites
115g /4oz /½ cup caster sugar
200g /7oz plain chocolate
175g /6oz /scant 1 cup Medjool dates,
   pitted and chopped
175g /6oz /1½ cups walnuts or pecan
   nuts, chopped
5ml /1 tsp vanilla essence, plus a few
   extra drops

1 Preheat the oven to 180°C/350°F/ Gas 4. Grease and base-line a 20cm/8in springform cake tin.

2 To make the frosting, mix together the fromage frais and mascarpone, add a few drops of vanilla essence and icing sugar to taste, then set aside.

3 Whisk the egg whites in a bowl until they form stiff peaks. Whisk in 30ml/2 tbsp of the caster sugar until the meringue is thick and glossy, then fold in the remainder.

4 Chop 175g/6oz of the chocolate. Carefully fold into the meringue with the dates, nuts and 5ml/1tsp of the vanilla essence. Pour into the prepared tin, spread level and bake for about 45 minutes, until risen around the edges.

5 Allow to cool in the tin for about 10 minutes, then turn out on to a wire rack. Peel off the lining paper and leave until completely cold. Swirl the frosting over the top of the torte.

6 Melt the remaining chocolate in a bowl over hot water. Spoon into a small paper piping bag, snip off the top and drizzle the chocolate over the torte. Chill before serving, cut in wedges.

BROWN BREAD ICE CREAM

Serves 6

50g/2oz/½ cup roasted and chopped
  hazelnuts, ground
75g/3oz/1½ cups wholemeal
  breadcrumbs
50g/2oz/4 tbsp demerara sugar
3 egg whites
115g/4oz/½ cup caster sugar
300ml/½ pint/1¼ cups double cream
few drops vanilla essence

For the sauce
225g/8oz blackcurrants
75g/3oz/6 tbsp caster sugar
15ml/1 tbsp crème de cassis
fresh mint sprigs, to decorate

1 Combine the hazelnuts and breadcrumbs on a baking sheet, then
sprinkle over the demerara sugar. Place
under a medium grill and cook, stirring,
until the mixture is crisp and evenly
browned. Leave to cool.

2 Whisk the egg whites in a bowl
until stiff, then gradually whisk in
the sugar until thick and glossy. Whip
the cream until it forms soft peaks and
fold into the meringue with the breadcrumb mixture and vanilla essence.

3 Spoon the mixture into a 1.2 litre/
2 pint/5 cup loaf tin. Smooth the
top level, then cover and freeze for
several hours, or until firm.

4 Meanwhile, make the sauce. Strip
the blackcurrants from their stalks
using a fork and put the blackcurrants
in a small bowl with the sugar. Toss
gently to mix and leave for 30 minutes.

5 Purée the blackcurrants in a blender
or food processor, then press
through a nylon sieve until smooth.
Add the crème de cassis and chill well.

6 To serve, turn out the ice cream
on to a plate and cut into slices.
Arrange each slice on a serving plate,
spoon over a little sauce and decorate
with fresh mint sprigs.

CAKES AND BAKES

British cakes are in a class of their own, but the type that is so well-known and loved today did not begin to be made until the mid-nineteenth century. Cake-making began as an off-shoot of bread-baking, and early cakes were leavened with yeast. Then, in America during the mid-1850s, a chemical raising agent was developed, which meant that lighter cakes could be produced. Plain cakes, gingerbreads and fruit cakes were popular for country suppers and high teas, while delicate sponges became fashionable among the middle classes. Besides the traditional cakes and teabreads, Scones, Drop Scones and Chelsea Buns make special tea-time treats to serve warm, while Shortbread and Melting Moments are handy to bake ahead and store in the biscuit tin.

CUSTARD LAYER CAKE

INGREDIENTS

Serves 8
225g/8oz/2 cups plain flour
15ml/1 tbsp baking powder
pinch of salt
115g/4oz/½ cup butter, at room
  temperature
200g/7oz/1 cup caster sugar
2 eggs
5ml/1 tsp vanilla essence
175ml/6fl oz/¾ cup milk

For the filling
250ml/8fl oz/1 cup milk
3 egg yolks
90g/3½oz/½ cup caster sugar
25g/1oz/¼ cup plain flour
15g/½oz/1 tbsp butter
15ml/1 tbsp brandy or 15ml/1 tsp
  vanilla essence

For the chocolate icing
25g/1oz plain chocolate
25g/1oz/2 tbsp butter or margarine
50g/2oz/½ cup icing sugar, plus extra
  for dusting
2.5ml/½ tsp vanilla essence
about 15ml/1 tbsp hot water

1 Preheat the oven to 190°C/375°F/
Gas 5. Grease two deep round cake
tins, and line the bases of each with
rounds of greased greaseproof paper.

2 Sift together the flour, baking
powder and salt. Beat the butter
and caster sugar together in a separate
bowl, until light and fluffy. Add the
eggs one at a time, beating well after
each addition. Stir in the vanilla
essence. Add the milk and dry
ingredients alternately, mixing only
enough to blend thoroughly. Do not
over-beat the mixture.

3 Divide the cake mixture between
the prepared tins and smooth the
top evenly. Bake for about 25 minutes,
until a skewer inserted in the centre
comes out clean.

4 Meanwhile, make the filling, heat
the milk in a small saucepan to
boiling point. Remove from the heat.

5 Whisk the egg yolks in a heatproof
mixing bowl. Gradually add the
sugar and continue whisking, until the
mixture is thick and pale yellow. Beat in
the sifted flour.

6 Pour the hot milk into the egg yolk
mixture in a steady stream, beating
constantly. Place the bowl over a pan of
boiling water, or pour the mixture into
the top of a double boiler. Heat, stirring
constantly, until thickened. Cook for a
further 2 minutes, then remove from the
heat. Stir in the butter and brandy or
vanilla essence. Set aside and leave until
cold, stirring frequently.

7 When the cakes have completely
cooled, place one on a serving plate
and carefully spread over the custard
filling in a thick layer using a large
palette knife. Place the other cake on
top. Smooth the edge of the custard
filling with a small palette knife or
teaspoon to remove excess custard and
give an attractive tidy finish to the cake.

8 To make the icing, melt the
chocolate with the butter or
margarine in the top of a double boiler
set over a pan of hot water. When
smooth, remove from the heat and beat
in the sugar to make a thick paste. Add
the vanilla essence, then beat in a little
of the hot water. If the icing does not
have a spreadable consistency, add
more water, 5ml/1 tsp at a time.

9 Using a large palette knife, spread
the icing evenly over the top of the
cake. Dust the top with icing sugar.
(Since it has a custard filling, store any
leftover cake in the fridge.)

WARM LEMON AND SYRUP CAKE

Serves 8
3 eggs
175g / 6oz / ¾ cup butter, softened
175g / 6oz / ¾ cup caster sugar
175g / 6oz / 1½ cups self-raising flour
50g / 2oz / ½ cup ground almonds
1.25ml / ¼ tsp freshly grated nutmeg
50g / 2oz candied lemon peel,
  finely chopped
grated rind of 1 lemon
30ml / 2 tbsp lemon juice
poached pears, to serve

For the syrup
175g / 6oz / ¾ cup caster sugar
juice of 3 lemons

1 Preheat the oven to 180°C / 350°F / Gas 4. Grease and base-line a deep, round 20cm / 8in cake tin.

2 Place all the cake ingredients in a large bowl and beat well for 2–3 minutes, until light and fluffy.

3 Tip the mixture into the prepared tin, spread level and bake for 1 hour, or until golden and firm to the touch.

4 Meanwhile, make the syrup. Put the sugar, lemon juice and 75ml / 5 tbsp water in a pan. Heat gently, stirring until the sugar has dissolved, then boil, without stirring, for 1–2 minutes.

5 Turn out the cake on to a plate with a rim. Prick the surface of the cake all over with a fork, then pour over the hot syrup. Leave to soak for about 30 minutes. Serve the cake warm with thin wedges of poached pears.

ONE-MIX CHOCOLATE SPONGE

For family teas and ever-open mouths, quick and easy favourites, like this chocolate cake, are invaluable.

INGREDIENTS

Serves 8–10

175g/6oz/¾ cup soft margarine, at room temperature
115g/4oz/½ cup caster sugar
50g/2oz/4 tbsp golden syrup
175g/6oz/1½ cups self-raising flour, sifted
45ml/3 tbsp cocoa, sifted
2.5ml/½ tsp salt
3 eggs, beaten
little milk (optional)
150ml/¼ pint/⅔ cup whipping cream
15–30ml/1–2 tbsp fine shred marmalade
sifted icing sugar, to decorate

1 Preheat the oven to 180°C/350°F/ Gas 4. Lightly grease or line two 18cm/7in sandwich tins. Place the margarine, sugar, syrup, flour, cocoa, salt and eggs in a large bowl or food processor and cream together until well blended. (In a processor use the slowest speed or frequent short bursts.)

COOK'S TIP

If you are filling up the freezer, this cake is ideal. Wrap the sponges in clear film and store for up to six months. Defrost for 2 hours before sandwiching the cake with the filling.

2 If the mixture seems a little thick, stir in 15–30ml/1–2 tbsp milk, until you have a soft dropping consistency. Spoon the mixture into the prepared tins and bake for about 30 minutes, changing shelves if necessary after 15 minutes, until the tops are just firm and the cakes are springy to the touch.

3 Leave the cakes to cool for 5 minutes, then remove from the tins and leave to cool completely on a wire rack.

4 Whip the cream and fold in the marmalade, then use to sandwich the two cakes together and sprinkle the top with sifted icing sugar.

CHOCOLATE CAKE

Ground lightly toasted hazelnuts and finely grated orange rind add an extra-special dimension to this luxurious moist cake.

INGREDIENTS

Makes about 10 slices
150g/5oz plain (semi-sweet)
  chocolate, chopped
115g/4oz/½ cup unsalted (sweet)
  butter, chopped
115g/4oz/½ cup caster (superfine)
  sugar
4 eggs, separated
115g/4oz ground lightly toasted
  hazelnuts (filberts)
50g/2oz/1 cup fresh breadcrumbs
grated rind of 1½ oranges
30ml/2 tbsp sieved (strained)
  marmalade, warmed
60ml/4 tbsp chopped hazelnuts
  (filberts), to decorate

For The Icing (Frosting)
150g/5oz plain (semi-sweet)
  chocolate, chopped
50g/2oz/4 tbsp butter, chopped

1 Preheat the oven to 180°C/350°F/ Gas 4. Butter a 23cm/9 in round cake tin (pan) and line the base with greaseproof (wax) paper.

2 Put the chocolate into a small bowl placed over a saucepan of hot water, leave until beginning to melt, then stir until smooth. Remove the bowl from the heat.

3 Beat the butter and sugar together until light and fluffy, then gradually beat in the egg yolks, beating well after each addition; do not worry if the mixture curdles slightly. Beat in the chocolate, then fold in the hazelnuts (filberts), breadcrumbs and orange rind. Whisk the egg whites until stiff but not dry, then fold into the chocolate mixture. Transfer to the cake tin (pan) and bake for 40–45 minutes, until just set in the centre.

4 Remove from the oven, cover with a damp tea towel for 5 minutes, then transfer to a wire rack until cold.

5 To make the icing (frosting), place the chocolate and butter in a bowl over a pan of hot water and stir until smooth. Leave until cool and thick. Spread the cake with marmalade, then spread over the icing (frosting). Scatter over the nuts, then leave to set.

NUTTY CARROT CAKE

Grated carrots are a very traditional addition to cakes and
puddings – they add both moisture and colour and produce a
moist cake that keeps well.

INGREDIENTS

Makes 8–10 slices
225g/8oz/1 cup butter
225g/8oz/generous 1 cup soft light
  brown sugar
4 eggs, separated
grated rind of 1 small orange
15ml/1 tbsp lemon juice
175g/6oz/1½ cups self-raising
  (self-rising) flour
5ml/1 tsp baking powder
50g/2oz/⅔ cup ground almonds
350g/12oz grated carrots
115g/4oz/1 cup walnut pieces

1 Preheat the oven to 180°C/350°F/
Gas 4. Grease and line a 20cm/8in
round cake tin (pan) with greaseproof
(wax) paper. Beat together the butter
and sugar until light and fluffy, then
beat in the egg yolks one at a time,
beating well after each addition.

2 Stir the orange rind and lemon juice
into the butter mixture, followed
by the flour, baking powder, ground
almonds, carrots and walnuts.

3 Whisk the egg whites until stiff but
not dry, then lightly fold into the
carrot mixture. Transfer to the tin
(pan), make a slight hollow in the
centre, then bake for about 1½ hours,
until risen and golden; cover the top if
it becomes too brown.

4 Leave the cake in the tin (pan) to
cool slightly, then turn out on to a
wire rack. Remove the lining paper and
leave to cool completely.

VARIATION
To make Courgette (Zucchini) And
Raisin Cake substitute grated
courgettes (zucchini) for the carrots
and use raisins in place of the
walnut pieces.

MADEIRA CAKE

In the nineteenth century, this cake was served mid-morning with a glass of Madeira wine.

Makes 8–10 slices
175g/6oz/¾ cup butter
175g/6oz/scant 1 cup caster (superfine) sugar
4 eggs, beaten
grated rind of 1 lemon
225g/8oz/2 cups self-raising (self-rising) flour
pinch of salt
2 strips of candied peel

1 Preheat the oven to 180°C/350°F/ Gas 4. Grease and line an 18cm/7in round cake tin (pan).

2 Beat together the butter and sugar until light and fluffy, then gradually beat in the eggs, adding the lemon rind and a little of the flour towards the end. Fold in the remaining flour and the salt, then turn into the prepared cake tin (pan) and smooth the surface.

3 Bake the cake for 30 minutes, until set, then carefully place the peel on the top. Bake for a further 10 minutes, then reduce the oven temperature to 160°C/325°F/Gas 3 and continue to bake until firm in the centre.

4 Leave the cake to cool slightly in the tin (pan), then turn on to a wire rack and carefully remove the lining paper.

MARMALADE TEABREAD

Makes 8–10 slices
200g/7oz/1¾ cups plain (all-purpose) flour
5ml/1 tsp baking powder
6.25ml/1¼ tsp ground cinnamon
90g/3½oz/7 tbsp butter or margarine
50g/2oz/3 tbsp soft light brown sugar
60ml/4 tbsp chunky orange marmalade
1 egg, beaten
about 45ml/3 tbsp milk
60ml/4 tbsp glacé icing and shreds of orange and lemon rind, to decorate

1 Preheat the oven to 160°C/325°F/ Gas 3. Butter a 900ml/1½ pint/3¾ cup loaf tin (pan), then line the base with greased greaseproof (wax) paper.

2 Sift the flour, baking powder and cinnamon together, toss in the butter, then rub in with your fingertips until the mixture resembles breadcrumbs. Stir in the sugar.

3 Mix together the marmalade, egg and most of the milk, then stir into the bowl to make a soft dropping consistency, adding more milk if necessary.

4 Transfer the mixture to the tin (pan) and bake for about 1¼ hours, until firm to the touch. Leave the cake to cool for 5 minutes, then turn on to a wire rack.

5 Carefully peel off the lining paper and leave the cake to cool completely. Drizzle the glacé icing over the top of the cake and decorate with the orange and lemon rinds.

PARKIN

The flavour of the cake will improve if it is stored in an airtight container for several days or a week before serving.

INGREDIENTS

Makes 16–20 squares
300ml/ ½ pint/ 1¼ cups milk
225g/8oz/ ¾ cup golden (corn) syrup
225g/8oz/ ¾ cup black treacle (molasses)
115g/4oz/ ½ cup butter or margarine, diced
50g/2oz/scant ¼ cup dark brown sugar
450g/1 lb/4 cups plain (all-purpose) flour
2.5ml/ ½ tsp bicarbonate of soda (baking soda)
6.25ml/1¼ tsp ground ginger
350g/12oz/4 cups medium oatmeal
1 egg, beaten
icing (confectioner's) sugar, to dust

1 Preheat the oven to 180°C/350°F/ Gas 4. Grease and line the base of a 20cm/8in square cake tin (pan). Gently heat together the milk, syrup, treacle (molasses), butter or margarine and sugar, stirring until smooth; do not boil.

2 Stir together the flour, bicarbonate of soda (baking soda), ginger and oatmeal. Make a well in the centre, pour in the egg, then slowly pour in the warmed mixture, stirring to make a smooth batter.

3 Pour the batter into the tin (pan) and bake for about 45 minutes, until firm to the touch. Cool slightly in the tin (pan), then cool completely on a wire rack. Cut into squares and dust with icing (confectioner's) sugar.

DORSET APPLE CAKE

Serve this fruity cake warm, and spread with butter if liked.

INGREDIENTS

Makes 6–8 slices
225g/8oz cooking apples, peeled, cored and chopped
juice of ½ lemon
225g/8oz/2 cups plain (all-purpose) flour
7.5ml/1½ tsp baking powder
115g/4oz/ ½ cup butter, diced
165g/5½ oz/scant 1 cup soft light brown sugar
1 egg, beaten
about 30–45 ml/2–3 tbsp milk, to mix
2.5ml/ ½ tsp ground cinnamon

1 Preheat the oven to 180°C/350°F/ Gas 4. Grease and line an 18cm/ 7 in round cake tin (pan).

2 Toss the apple with the lemon juice and set aside. Sift the flour and baking power, rub in the butter, until the mixture resembles breadcrumbs.

3 Stir in 115g/4oz/ ¾ cup of the sugar, the apple and the egg, and mix well, adding sufficient milk to make a soft dropping consistency.

4 Transfer the dough to the prepared tin (pan). In a bowl mix together the remaining sugar and the cinnamon. Sprinkle over the cake mixture, then bake for 45–50 minutes, until golden. Leave to cool in the tin (pan) for 10 minutes, then transfer to a wire rack.

SHORTBREAD

Traditionally the shortbread dough is pressed into decorative wooden moulds, then turned out for baking.

INGREDIENTS

Makes 6–8 wedges
115g/4oz/½ cup unsalted (sweet) butter
50g/2oz/4 tbsp caster (superfine) sugar
115g/4oz/1 cup plain (all-purpose) flour
50g/2oz/4 tbsp rice flour

1 Preheat the oven to 160°C/325°F/ Gas 3. Place a 15cm/6in plain flan ring on a baking (cookie) sheet.

2 Beat the butter and sugar together until light and fluffy. Stir in the plain (all-purpose) flour and the rice flour, then knead lightly until smooth.

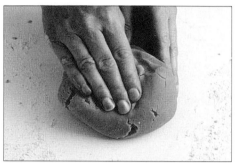

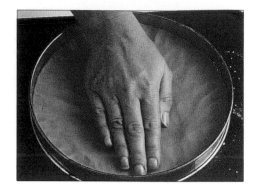

3 Press the dough evenly into the flan ring, then lift the flan ring away. Crimp around the edges of the dough using your thumb and first finger. Prick the surface of the round with a fork, then mark into 6 or 8 wedges.

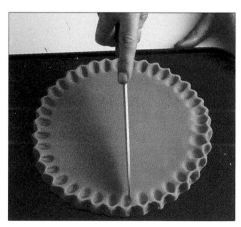

4 Bake the shortbread dough for 40 minutes, until pale biscuit coloured and just firm to the touch.

5 Leave the shortbread to cool for a few minutes, then carefully transfer to a wire rack to cool completely. To serve, break the shortbread into wedges along the marked lines.

COOK'S TIP
If you haven't a flan ring, then just roll out the dough until a little larger than a 15cm/6in round, then place a 15cm/6in plate on top and trim the edge neatly with a sharp knife. Remove the plate, crimp the edge of the shortbread and transfer to the baking sheet.

SIMNEL CAKE

This Easter-tide cake keeps well and is best made about six weeks ahead. The balls are said to represent Jesus' faithful apostles.

INGREDIENTS

Makes 8–10 slices

175g/6oz/¾ cup butter
175g/6oz/scant 1 cup soft brown sugar
3 large eggs
225g/8oz/2 cups plain (all-purpose) flour
2.5ml/½ tsp ground cinnamon
2.5ml/½ tsp freshly grated nutmeg
150g/5oz/1 cup currants
150g/5oz/¾ cup sultanas (white raisins)
150g/5oz/¾ cup raisins
75g/3oz/generous ½ cup glacé (candied) cherries, washed, dried and quartered
75g/3oz/generous ½ cup mixed (candied) peel, chopped
grated rind of 1 large lemon
450g/1 lb almond paste
caster (superfine) sugar, for dusting
1 egg white, lightly beaten

1 Preheat the oven to 160°C/325°F/ Gas 3. Grease and line an 18cm/7 in round cake tin (pan). Tie a double layer of brown paper round the outside.

2 Beat the butter and sugar together until pale and fluffy, then gradually beat in the eggs, beating well after each addition. Lightly fold the flour, spices, dried fruits, cherries, mixed (candied) peel and lemon rind into the egg mixture then spoon half the mixture into the tin (pan).

3 Roll half the almond paste to a 16cm/6½ in round on a surface dusted with caster (superfine) sugar. Place the round in the cake tin (pan).

4 Spoon the remaining cake mixture into the tin and bake for 1 hour. Reduce the oven temperature to 150°C/ 300°F/Gas 2 and bake for 2 hours. Leave to cool for 1 hour in the cake tin (pan), then cool on a wire rack.

5 Brush the cake top with egg white. Roll out half the remaining almond paste to a 19cm/7½ in round, place on the cake and crimp. Roll the remaining paste into 11 balls and fix with egg white. Brush the paste with more egg white and grill (broil) until browned.

DATE AND NUT MALTLOAF

INGREDIENTS

Makes 2 x 450g/1lb loaves

300g/11oz/2 cups strong plain flour
275g/10oz/2 cups strong plain whole-meal flour
5ml/1 tsp salt
75g/3oz/6 tbsp soft brown sugar
1 sachet easy-blend dried yeast
50g/2oz/4 tbsp butter or margarine
15ml/1 tbsp black treacle
60ml/4 tbsp malt extract
scant 250ml/8 floz/1 cup tepid milk
115g/4oz/½ cup chopped dates
50g/2oz/½ cup chopped nuts
75g/3oz/½ cup sultanas
75g/3oz/½ cup raisins
30ml/2 tbsp clear honey, to glaze

1 Sift the flours and salt into a large bowl, then tip in the wheat flakes that are caught in the sieve. Stir in the sugar and yeast.

2 Put the butter or margarine in a small pan with the treacle and malt extract. Stir over a low heat until melted. Leave to cool, then combine with the milk.

3 Stir the liquid into the dry ingredients and knead thoroughly for 15 minutes until the dough is elastic. (If you have a dough blade on your food processor, follow the manufacturers' instructions for timings.)

4 Knead in the fruits and nuts. Transfer the dough to an oiled bowl, cover with clear film and leave in a warm place for about 1½ hours, until the dough has doubled in size.

5 Grease two 450g/1lb loaf tins. Knock back the dough and knead lightly. Divide in half, form into loaves and place in the tins. Cover and leave in a warm place for about 30 minutes, until risen. Meanwhile, preheat the oven to 190°C/375°F/Gas 5.

6 Bake for 35–40 minutes, until well risen and sounding hollow when tapped underneath. Cool on a wire rack. Brush with honey while warm.

STICKY GINGERBREAD

Makes 1 loaf
175g/6oz/1½ cups plain flour
10ml/2 tsp ground ginger
2.5ml/½ tsp mixed spice
2.5ml/½ tsp bicarbonate of soda
30ml/2 tbsp black treacle
30ml/2 tbsp golden syrup
75g/3oz/⅝ cup soft dark brown sugar
75g/3oz/6 tbsp butter
1 egg
15ml/1 tbsp milk
15ml/1 tbsp orange juice
2 pieces stem ginger, finely chopped
50g/2oz/½ cup sultanas
5 ready-to-eat apricots, finely chopped
45ml/3 tbsp icing sugar
10ml/2 tsp lemon juice

1 Preheat the oven to 160°C/325°F/ Gas 3. Grease and line a 1kg/2lb loaf tin. Sift the flour, spices and bicarbonate of soda into a bowl.

2 Place the treacle, syrup, sugar and butter in a pan and heat gently until the butter has melted.

3 In a separate small bowl beat the egg, milk and orange juice together.

5 When cooked, remove from the oven, and leave to cool in the tin. Mix the icing sugar with the lemon juice in a bowl and beat until smooth. Drizzle the icing back and forth over the top of the gingerbread, leave to set, then cut into thick slices to serve.

4 Add the syrup, egg mixture, chopped ginger, sultanas and apricots to the dry ingredients and stir well. Spoon into the prepared tin and level out. Bake in the oven for about 50 minutes, or until the gingerbread is well risen and a skewer pierced through the centre comes out clean.

TANGY LEMON CAKE

INGREDIENTS

Makes about 10 slices
175g/6oz/¾ cup butter
175g/6oz/scant 1 cup caster (superfine) sugar
3 eggs, beaten
175g/6oz/1½ cups self-raising (self-rising) flour
grated rind of 1 orange
grated rind of 1 lemon

For The Syrup
juice of 2 lemons
115g/4oz/generous ½ cup caster (superfine) sugar

1 Preheat the oven to 180°C/350°F/ Gas 4. Grease a 900g/2 lb loaf tin (pan).

2 Beat the butter and sugar together until light and fluffy, then gradually beat in the eggs. Fold in the flour and the orange and lemon rinds.

3 Turn the cake mixture into the cake tin (pan) and bake for 1¼-1½ hours, until set in the centre, risen and golden.

4 Remove the cake from the oven, but leave it in the tin (pan).

5 To make the syrup, gently heat the sugar in the lemon juice until melted, then boil for 15 seconds. Pour the syrup over the cake and leave to cool.

CHELSEA BUNS

INGREDIENTS

Makes 12
225g/8oz/2 cups strong white flour
½ tsp salt
40g/1½oz/3 tbsp unsalted (sweet) butter
7.5ml/1½ tsp easy-blend yeast
120ml/4 fl oz/½ cup milk
1 egg, beaten
75g/3oz/½ cup mixed dried fruit
25g/1oz/2½ tbsp chopped mixed (candied) peel
50g/2oz/3 tbsp soft light brown sugar
clear honey, to glaze

1 Sift the flour and salt into a bowl, then rub in 25g/1oz/2 tbsp of the butter until the mixture resembles breadcrumbs.

2 Stir in the yeast and make a well in the centre. Slowly pour the milk and egg into the well, stirring the ingredients together, then beat until the dough leaves the sides of the bowl clean.

3 Knead the dough until smooth and elastic. Place in an oiled bowl, cover and leave at room temperature until doubled in volume. Transfer the dough to a floured surface, then roll to a rectangle about 30 x 23cm/12 x 9in.

4 Mix the dried fruits, peel and sugar. Melt the remaining butter and brush over the dough. Scatter over the fruit mixture, leaving a 2.5cm/1in border. Starting at a long side, roll up the dough. Seal the edges, then cut into 12 slices.

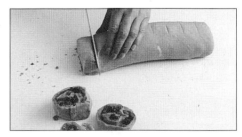

5 Place the slices, cut side up, in a greased 18cm/7in square tin (pan). Cover and leave at room temperature until doubled in size.

6 Preheat the oven to 190°C/375°F/ Gas 5. Bake for 30 minutes, until a rich golden brown. Brush the tops with honey and leave to cool slightly in the tin (pan) before turning out.

DUNDEE CAKE

INGREDIENTS

Serves 16–20

175g/6oz/¾ cup butter

175g/6oz/scant ¾ cup soft light
  brown sugar

3 eggs

225g/8oz/2 cups plain flour

10ml/2 tsp baking powder

5ml/1 tsp ground cinnamon

2.5ml/½ tsp ground cloves

1.5ml/¼ tsp ground nutmeg

225g/8oz/1⅓ cups sultanas

175g/6oz/1 cup raisins

175g/6oz//1 cup glacé cherries, halved

115g/4oz/¾ cup chopped mixed peel

50g/2oz/⅓ cup blanched almonds,
  roughly chopped

grated rind of 1 lemon

30ml/2 tbsp brandy

75g/3oz/⅔ cup whole blanched almonds

1 Preheat oven to 160°C/325°F/Gas 3. Grease and line a 20cm/8in round, deep cake tin. Cream the butter and sugar together. Add the eggs, one at a time, beating well after each addition.

2 Sift the flour, baking powder and spices together. Fold into the creamed mixture alternately with the remaining ingredients, apart from the whole almonds, until evenly blended.

3 Transfer to the prepared tin, smooth the surface, making a small dip in the centre. Decorate the top of the cake mixture by pressing the almonds in decreasing circles over the entire surface. Bake for 2–2¼ hours until a skewer, inserted in the centre, comes out clean.

4 Remove from the oven, cool in the tin for 30 minutes, and transfer to a wire rack to cool completely.

> **COOK'S TIP**
> All rich fruit cakes improve in flavour if left in a cool place for up to three months. Wrap the cake in greaseproof paper and a double layer of foil.

DE LUXE MINCEMEAT TART

The mincemeat can be made up and kept in the fridge for up to two weeks. It can be used to make individual mince pies.

INGREDIENTS

Serves 8
225g/8oz/2 cups plain flour
10ml/2 tsp ground cinnamon
50g/2oz/⅔ cup walnuts, finely ground
115g/4oz/½ cup butter
50g/2oz/4 tbsp caster sugar, plus extra
   for dusting
1 egg
2 drops of vanilla essence
15ml/1 tbsp cold water

For The Mincemeat
2 dessert apples, peeled, cored and
   coarsely grated
225g/8oz/1⅓ cups raisins
115g/4oz no-soak dried apricots,
   chopped
115g/4oz no-soak dried figs or prunes,
   chopped
225g/8oz green grapes, halved and
   seeded
50g/2oz/½ cup chopped almonds
finely grated rind of 1 lemon
30ml/2 tbsp lemon juice
30ml/2 tbsp brandy or port
¼ tsp mixed spice
115g/4oz/generous ½ cup soft light
   brown sugar
25g/1oz/2 tbsp butter, melted

1 To make the pastry, put the flour, cinnamon and walnuts in a food processor. Add the butter and process until the mixture resembles fine bread-crumbs. Turn into a bowl and stir in the sugar. Using a fork, beat the egg with the vanilla essence and water. Gradually stir the egg mixture into the dry ingredients. Gather together with your fingertips to form a soft, pliable dough. Knead briefly on a lightly floured surface until smooth; then wrap the dough in clear film and chill it for 30 minutes.

2 Mix all the mincemeat ingredients together thoroughly in a bowl.

3 Cut-one-third off the pastry and reserve it for the lattice. Roll out the remainder and use it to line a 23cm/9in, loose-based flan tin. Take care to push the pastry well into the edges and make a 5mm/¼in rim around the top edge. With a rolling pin, roll off the excess pastry to neaten the edge. Fill the pastry case with the mincemeat.

4 Roll out the remaining pastry and cut it into 1cm/½in strips. Arrange the strips in a lattice over the top of the filling, wet the joins and press them together well. Chill for 30 minutes.

5 Preheat the oven to 190°C/375°F/ Gas 5. Place a baking sheet in the oven to preheat. Brush the pastry with water and dust it with caster sugar. Bake it on the baking sheet for 30–40 minutes. Transfer to a wire rack and leave to cool for 15 minutes. Then care-fully remove the flan tin. Serve warm or cold, with sweetened whipped cream, if desired.

FRUIT AND NUT TURNOVERS

── INGREDIENTS ──

Makes 16

*350g/12oz/2 cups mixed dried fruit,
   such as apricots and prunes*
75g/3oz/¹/₂ cup raisins
115g/4oz/¹/₂ cup soft light brown sugar
*65g/2¹/₂oz/¹/₂ cup pine nuts or chopped
   almonds*
2.5ml/¹/₂ tsp ground cinnamon
oil, for frying
*45ml/3 tbsp caster sugar mixed with
   5ml/1 tsp ground cinnamon, for
   sprinkling*

For the pastry

225g/8oz/2 cups plain flour
1.25ml/¹/₄ tsp baking powder
1.25ml/¹/₄ tsp salt
10ml/2 tsp caster sugar
50g/2oz/4 tbsp unsalted butter, chilled
25g/1oz/2 tbsp white cooking fat
*120–175ml/4–6fl oz/¹/₂–³/₄ cup
   iced water*

1 To make the pastry, sift the flour, baking powder, salt and sugar into a bowl. With a pastry blender or two knives, cut the butter and cooking fat into the flour until the mixture resembles fine breadcrumbs. Sprinkle with 120ml/4fl oz/¹/₂ cup iced water and mix until the dough holds together. If the dough is too crumbly, add a little more water, 15ml/1 tbsp at a time.

2 Gather the dough into a ball and gently flatten into a round. Place in a polythene bag, seal and chill for at least 30 minutes.

3 Place all the dried fruit in a saucepan and add cold water to cover. Bring to the boil, then simmer gently for about 30 minutes, until the fruit is soft enough to purée.

4 Drain the fruit and place in a food processor or blender. Process until smooth, then return the fruit purée to the saucepan. Add the brown sugar and cook for about 5 minutes, stirring constantly, until thick. Remove the pan from the heat and stir in the pine nuts or almonds, and the ground cinnamon. Leave the mixture to cool.

5 Roll out the chilled pastry to 3mm/¹/₈in thickness. Stamp out rounds with a 10cm/4in pastry cutter. Re-roll the pastry trimmings and cut out more rounds to make sixteen in all.

> **COOK'S TIP**
> The pastry and the filling can both be made up to two days in advance and chilled until needed.

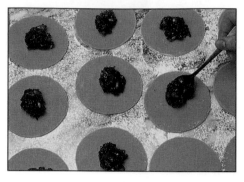

6 Place a spoonful of the fruit in the centre of each pastry round.

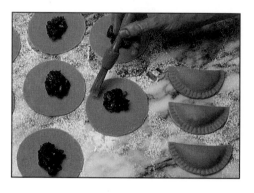

7 Moisten the edge of the pastry rounds with water and fold over to form a half-moon shape. Crimp the rounded edge with a fork.

8 Put a 1cm/¹/₂in layer of oil in a heavy frying pan and heat until hot, but not smoking (to test, drop a scrap of pastry into the oil; if the oil sizzles, it is hot enough). Add the turnovers, a few at a time, and fry for about 1¹/₂ minutes on each side, until golden.

9 Drain the turnovers briefly on kitchen paper, then sprinkle with the cinnamon sugar. Serve warm.

DROP SCONES

Makes 8–10

115g/4oz/1 cup plain (all-purpose)
flour
5ml/1 tsp bicarbonate of soda (baking
soda)
5ml/1 tsp cream of tartar
25g/1oz/2 tbsp butter, diced
1 egg, beaten
about 150ml/¼ pint/⅔ cup milk

1 Lightly grease a griddle or heavy-based frying pan, then preheat it.

2 Sift the flour, bicarbonate of soda (baking soda) and cream of tartar together, then rub in the butter until the mixture resembles breadcrumbs. Make a well in the centre, then stir in the egg and sufficient milk to give a thick cream consistency.

3 Drop spoonfuls of the mixture, spaced slightly apart, on to the griddle or frying pan. Cook over a steady heat for 2–3 minutes, until bubbles rise to the surface and burst.

4 Turn the scones over and cook for a further 2–3 minutes, until golden underneath. Place the cooked scones in between the folds of a tea towel while cooking the remaining batter. Serve warm, with butter and honey.

> COOK'S TIP
> Placing the cooked scones in a folded tea towel keeps them soft and moist.

SCONES

Makes 10–12

225g/8oz/2 cups plain (all-purpose) flour
15ml/1 tbsp baking powder
50g/2oz/4tbsp butter, diced
1 egg, beaten
75ml/5 tbsp milk
beaten egg, to glaze

1 Preheat the oven to 220°C/425°F/ Gas 7. Butter a baking (cookie) sheet. Sift the flour and baking powder together, then rub in the butter.

2 Make a well in the centre of the flour mixture, add the egg and milk and mix to a soft dough using a round-bladed knife.

3 Turn out the scone dough on to a floured surface, knead very lightly until smooth.

4 Roll out the dough to about a 2cm/ ¾in thickness and cut into 10 or 12 rounds using a 5cm/2in plain or fluted cutter dipped in flour.

5 Transfer to the baking (cookie) sheet, brush with egg, then bake for about 8 minutes, until risen and golden. Cool slightly on a wire rack then serve with butter, jam and cream.

MELTING MOMENTS

These biscuits (cookies) are very crisp and light – and they melt in your mouth.

Makes 16–20
40g/1½oz/3 tbsp butter or margarine
65g/2½oz/5 tbsp lard (shortening)
75g/3oz/6 tbsp caster (superfine) sugar
½ egg, beaten
*few drops of vanilla or almond essence
   (extract)*
*150g/5oz/1¼ cups self-raising (self-
   rising) flour*
rolled oats, for coating
4–5 glacé (candied) cherries, quartered

1 Preheat the oven to 180°C/350°F/ Gas 4. Beat together the butter or margarine, lard (shortening) and sugar, then gradually beat in the egg and vanilla or almond essence (extract).

2 Stir the flour into the beaten mixture, then roll into 16–20 small balls in your hands.

3 Spread the rolled oats on a sheet of greaseproof (wax) paper and toss the balls in them to coat evenly.

4 Place the balls, spaced slightly apart, on 2 baking (cookie) sheets, place a piece of cherry on top of each and bake for 15–20 minutes, until lightly browned.

5 Allow the biscuits (cookies) to cool for a few minutes before transferring to a wire rack to cool completely.

EASTER BISCUITS (COOKIES)

Makes 16–18
115g/4oz/½ cup butter or margarine
*75g/3oz/6 tbsp caster (superfine)
   sugar, plus extra for sprinkling*
1 egg, separated
*200g/7oz/1¾ cups plain (all-purpose)
   flour*
2.5ml/½ tsp ground mixed spice
2.5ml/½ tsp ground cinnamon
50g/2oz/scant ½ cup currants
*15ml/1 tbsp chopped mixed (candied)
   peel*
15–30ml/1–2 tbsp milk

1 Preheat the oven to 200°C/400°F/ Gas 6. Lightly grease two baking (cookie) sheets.

2 Beat together the butter or margarine and sugar until light and fluffy, then beat in the egg yolk.

3 Sift the flour and spices over the egg mixture, then fold in with the currants and peel, adding sufficient milk to mix to a fairly soft dough.

4 Turn the dough on to a floured surface, knead lightly until just smooth, then roll out using a floured rolling pin, to about 5mm/¼ in thick. Cut the dough into rounds using a 5cm/2in fluted biscuit (cookie) cutter. Transfer the rounds to the baking sheets and bake for 10 minutes.

5 Beat the egg white, then brush over the biscuits (cookies). Sprinkle with caster (superfine) sugar and return to the oven for a further 10 minutes, until golden. Transfer to a wire rack to cool.

INDEX

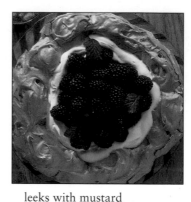

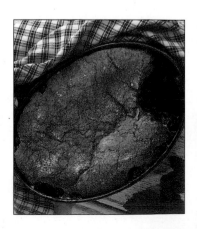